MW00454477

Mutual Blessing

Mutual Blessing

Discovering the Ultimate Destiny of Creation

Daniel C. Juster, Th. D.

Lederer Books
A division of
Messianic Jewish Publishers
Clarksville, MD 21029

Copyright © 2013 by Daniel Juster

All rights reserved. No part of this publication may be reproduced, stored in a retrieval system, or transmitted in any form or by any means without prior written permission of the publisher, except for brief reviews in magazines or as quotations in another work when full attribution is given

All scripture comes from the *Complete Jewish Bible* (CJB) translation by David H. Stern unless otherwise stated. Copyright © 1998. All rights reserved. Used by permission of Messianic Jewish Publishers.

16 15 14 13   4 3 2 1

ISBN-13: 978-1-936716-74-6

Library of Congress Control Number: 2013952869
Printed in the United States of America
Cover art: Mosaic in Caesarea Maritima - the ancient roman city Israel
by Karol Kozlowski, BigStock Photo 49371914

Lederer Books
A division of
Messianic Jewish Publishers
6120 Day Long Lane
Clarksville, MD 21029

Distributed by
Messianic Jewish Resources Int'l
Order line: (800) 410-7367
lederer@messianicjewish.net
www.messianicjewish.net

Contents

Introduction

This book presents a foundation for theology through the concept of mutual blessing. If the Kingdom of God is the most basic and integrating concept of biblical theology, then the concept of mutual blessing is the most basic to describing how this Kingdom, which is a kingdom of love, functions. God has created the universe to be interdependent. We see this through creation distinctions. God and creation are distinct. It is by creation distinctions that mutual blessing though interdependence is possible. The foundation of mutual blessing is God's love. Love is to permeate the creation.

This book is not a scholarly defense, providing every possible footnote and reference but rather a reflection from Holy Spirit inspiration. However, there is scholarly support. Additionally, you can search the libraries and gather footnotes. The necessary scholarly reading has been done, and I will sometimes refer to scholars. It may seem as if I make assertions without adequate proof. However, my purpose is more inspirational than apologetic. I am asserting what I believe to be fruitful ideas and why, and I provide some books as foundational references. Three scholars or researchers were a great influence for this book. Their seminal ideas were the inspiration. First was Bill Ligon who nearly completed a doctorate dissertation in theology on the subject of blessing. New and pressing pastoral responsibilities kept him from finishing his research. His teaching tapes are valuable summaries of his research. He emphasized conveying blessings directly through words. He drew heavily upon Rabbinic Judaism's preservation of the meaning of blessings. The writings of Claus Westermann, a noted biblical scholar, were significant in influencing Bill Ligon's thought. I recommend pursuing Westermann's writings. There is also an excellent book by Methodist theologian, R. Kendall Soulen, *The God of Israel and Christian Theology*.[1] Soulen argues that most Christian theology emphasizes redemption, which causes the creation order to be overlooked. His work addresses why the Messiah died and rose again. What is the full purpose in restoration that will be attained on the basis of his death and resurrection? It is an order of mutual blessing that will permeate the creation.

When we speak of blessing, we mean an enrichment of the life of another. It is an enrichment of the other without negative repercussions for the one who enriches. Much of what people covet is not truly enriching from *God's point of view*. But true blessing is enrichment from *God's point of view*, not necessarily what sinful people selfishly desire.

The meaning of mutual enrichment is often best revealed in the world of Art. Artists are God's gifts with the purpose to awaken us to the multiple orders of mutual blessing. Therefore

---

1. R. Kendall Soulen, *The God of Israel and Christian Theology*, Minneapolis, Fortress Press, 1996.

I will add hymns, pictures, poems, and psalms to open hearts to the grandeur of God's order. This is a book for meditation.

We trust that this book inspires and enlightens. It is Messianic Jewish in perspective, but not myopic. It is a Jewish rooted understanding in the sense of seeking the original context for understanding the Scriptures. This is important for all.

Chapter I:

The Order of Creation, Genesis One

"**I**n the beginning God created the heavens and the earth" (Genesis 1:1). The book of Genesis begins with this amazingly stark statement. Classical Judaism and Christianity based their view of reality, Theism, upon this chapter. Theism argues that God did not make the universe from previously existing eternal substance (as in Plato's Timeaus or as in varieties of Pan-en-theism where all is in God). Nor are we to think of the Universe as God (Pantheism). Classical interpreters saw in the Hebrew word "bara" an amazing concept, creation from nothing. In one sense, this is not coherent. How can one conceive of making something out of nothing? However, in another sense, the concept of "bara" can be seen as making a distinction between the Creator and the World, his creation. We are on the creation side of this distinction; human thought cannot penetrate beyond creation to the Creator side. If we begin to conceive of God as using material substance, as we know it, to create, we are bound to fall into error. God's being is not diminished in creating. We are not to think of God creating out of His body, or out of the substance of light that emanates from his being (as in Gnostic speculations and sometimes even in cabalistic thought). Genesis 1:1 states that the creation is brought forth by God's Word. As the Psalmist said, "By the Word of the Lord were the heavens made, and their story host by the breath of his mouth. . . . He spoke and it came to be; He commanded, and it stood forth." (Psalm 33:6, 9).

Some have not been able to come to terms with the uniqueness of the Genesis account. They assume it must really be more like the accounts of the nations. E. A. Speiser in the *Anchor Bible Commentary on Genesis*[1] interprets the verse to say that when God began to create, the earth was without form. In his interpretation, the substance already existed. Accordingly he maintains God worked on a previously existing substance. However, it is not so in the other Bible texts. Genesis describes no action upon substance, but speech that creates the heavens and the earth, including the substance.

The Spirit of God is described as hovering over the newly created being of the heavens and the earth—as a mother hen broods over her eggs. Then God says, "Let there be light" (Genesis 1:3). God separated light from darkness; He called the light day and the darkness night. We immediately see herein the first distinction in the created order. Blessing will come to all sentient beings because of the distinction between light and dark. Light and dark are interdependent. Without dark, light is blinding, and no creation distinctions would be visible to the eye. Shadows and levels of brilliance are keys to

---

1. E. A. Speiser, Genesis, Anchor Bible Series, New Haven, Yale University Press, 1963.

sight, and only the interdependence of light and dark for sight makes this possible. God saw this and declared it good. So we find the repeated statement after several periods of creation. What can it mean for God to declare, "It is good." By what standard? It can only mean that God's creation was a blessing or enrichment to His own life, but not in the sense of fulfilling need from the human perspective. However, once God decided to create, his creation is rooted in a foundational purpose: to bring him blessing, to enrich his life.

On the second day of creation, God separates the waters above from the waters below. Then on the third day, God separates the water from the dry land. Next God brought forth vegetation of all kinds. Again, God calls the work of the third day good. It must be that his own life is again enriched by the beauty, the glory, and the intricacy of plant life.

On the fourth day, God orders the sun, moon and stars in relationship to the earth. This is the beginning of the measurement of time as we know it. Many godly thinkers have seen this point. Time as we know it in human society only came into being on the fourth day. It was not that the sun and the moon did not exist before, but that the earth, sun and moon are brought into relationship to months and years where the rotation of the earth measures 24 hours. The moon is seen at night, the reflected light, and the sun is seen by day. The stars are also so ordered at this time. Again, the order of creation is a blessing to God. He calls it good.

By the forth day we see the distinctions between light and darkness connected to the sun as the light producer and the moon as reflected light. We also see the distinction between the inanimate and the animate. Only on the fifth day do we see animal life brought forth. We read of birds and all kinds of sea creatures. Even sea monsters were created. Here we read the first word of blessing. "God blessed them, saying, 'Be fruitful and multiply, and fill the waters in the sea, and let birds multiply on the earth'" (Genesis 1:22). Before this word of blessing, God again declared that what He had created was good. How could it be any other? Again, His own life is enriched by the work of his creation. The blessing is connected to the command to be fruitful and multiply. This further enriches God. I should note that we cannot understand how his creation enriches God except by human analogies of the artist enriched by his own creation or those who love being enriched by loving and being loved. We simply have to accept that God is declaring that he is enriched or blessed.

The sixth day brings a further advancement. God brings forth every kind of land animal, creeping things and cattle, and all kinds of living creatures. God saw that it was good (Genesis 1:24, 25). Genesis 1:26 brings us to an apex of creation, for we read that "God created man in his own image ... male and female He created them." God commands them to be fruitful and multiply; to fill the earth and subdue it. Karl Barth in his *Church Dogmatics*[2] saw here an allusion to God's own triune life for only a relationship can express the image of God. Others have disputed this. Some take the words, *"Let us create man in our image,"* as indicating the same relational dimensions. *"Human beings are given charge to rule over the fish of the sea, the birds of the sky and over every living creature."*

---

2.   Karl Barth, *Church Dogmatics,* translated by Geoffrey Bromiley, *Vol. III*: chapter, 2. Edinburg: T. & T. Clark, 1960

Historically, theologians disputed the meaning of being created in the image of God. Does this mean that man is like God both in the soul and body so that he looks like God as in Mormonism? Some have argued that the image is in man's thinking, his rationality. Others have said it is in his moral nature. There is another group who define it as man's ability to love. None of these answers are correct. They are partial at best. It is now quite certain from archaeological study that the image of God is to be defined in the terms of the ancient kings and their ruling regents. When a king sent his regent to rule a vassal people, or a territory of his kingdom, he was called his image. The people were to see the king's regent and obey as if the regent were the king. A good regent must have the attributes of his king to rule as the king would desire. Man's being created in the image of God includes all the capacities that man needs to rule this earth wisely as God's regent or authority upon the earth. It includes his capacity to think, to intuit, to be in fellowship with God, to love, to worship, to make moral distinctions, and to feel. Yes, right passion and desire are necessary for this rule. Man is not a robot or a computer. The whole man is in God's image according to his calling or function.

One of the key aspects of man's being in God's image is the ability to worship God. God desires our fellowship. In worship, we acknowledge the greatness of God who is beyond our thoughts and imagination. We enter into expressions of love, submission, adoration and praise. We were made to worship. He in turn gives us the greatest gift that man can know, his very own presence. He is enriched in fellowship with his human creature, and we are enriched by his presence, for "at his right hand are pleasures forevermore" (Ps. 16:11).

Finally, God ties himself permanently to the human race through the incarnation of Yeshua. In the incarnation, we see one who is both God and man, divinity and humanity in one person. The incarnation is God's choice for mutual interdependence in an order of mutual blessing between God himself and the human race. The incarnation is more than the means for saving humanity, though it of course includes this. It is an everlasting commitment on God's part. How so? It is God's manifestation of his unity with humanity and a commitment to forever preserve the human race as in everlasting connection to himself. It is a supreme manifestation of God's love. There is now mutual blessing through one who bridges the creator and the human creature.

In Genesis, we see here the great distinctions between God and man, male and female, man and nature, and God and nature. First of all, man is not God. He is a created being, not an Uncreated Infinite Being. As such, he is created to be submitted to God and finds himself under the commandment to be fruitful, to multiply and to rule. God delegates rulership over this earth to man. In addition, man is both part of nature and distinct from nature. By the gift of language, (God spoke the World into existence) man shares God's ability to understand and to be creative. Man is to rule nature wisely. If man will rule nature wisely, it will bring him and nature great enrichment. We will expand this in a later chapter. Nature is not seen as perfected, but man is given opportunity to bring nature to its maturity. He is to be blessed by nature and to bless nature. *Man and nature are distinct for mutual blessing and interdependence.* Though in one sense man is part of nature, in another sense, he transcends nature.

Former Vice President, Al Gore, has written against this Genesis chapter in his book *Earth in Balance*[3] (ghost written by Jeremy Rifkin). He argues that this passage gives man the right to destroy nature and to not live in proper respect for nature. This is a real misunderstanding. Man does have the freedom to sin and to destroy both himself and nature. However, the present passage is a call to responsible stewardship. Man is to rule the earth in such a way that it brings blessing to God. He is to rule according to God's laws, both by the written word of Torah and by the laws of good science. This passage is called the dominion mandate. God will hold us accountable for our stewardship. A severe judgment awaits those who destroy the earth (Rev. 11:18). Can one really believe that the vagaries of New Age thought (embraced by Mr. Gore) really will produce a greater motivation to good stewardship? Will we respect the earth more if we see it as God or part of God and when God is so vaguely defined that he cannot morally hold us accountable? Do we see Hindu religion and the caste system in India as having produced good ecology? The Bible, rightly understood, is pro-ecology. However, it does not permit the deification of nature. Only in a biblical context will there be patience for good science rather than the worship of nature that will end up destroying what is worshipped through junk science. Again, as Rabbi Abraham Heschel says, "The Earth is our sister, not our mother."[4] When nature is deified, emotional decisions are made that do not take into account the long term consequences of rash actions.

---

3. Al Gore, *Earth in the Balance, Ecology and the Human Spirit*, Houghton Mifflin, Boston, 1992.
4. Abraham Joshua Heschel, *Man is Not Alone*, Farrar, Straus, Giroux, New York, 1952, 115.

For example, radical environmentalists have eliminated incandescent light bulbs to cut polluting energy. That is a good goal, but they did not take into account the danger of mercury disposal in fluorescent bulbs! By seeking to free us of fossil fuel, corn production for fuel is subsidized causing a terrible rise in food prices. Again and again intervention in markets is not well thought out because of the religious fervor to do something.

In addition, we need to see that nature is fallen. Nature is, in part, raw material for man's perfecting. As wonderful as it is, it is in need of redemption. Nature is red in tooth and claw as the old saying goes. Tragic natural disasters take place. Therefore we read that, "The whole creation labors ... eagerly waiting for the redemption ... and the manifestation of the sons of God" (Romans 8:19-22). Nature itself was consigned to futility because of the fall. Man and nature are so tied that nature reflects that fall and becomes the proper environment for a fallen man. With all its beauty and glory, nature is often insensitive to man; it is harsh and destructive.

Then there is war. Nature and man together can bring great suffering. As Paul says, the whole creation groans and travails (Romans).

So we come to the end of the sixth day and we read that "God saw all that He had made and behold it was very good" (1:31). Indeed, at the end of the sixth day, God sees the great richness, variety, complexity, beauty, and interdependence of the creation order, and man as his regent. He sees it to be very good. God now enjoys the whole of it.

Psalm 104

1 Praise the LORD, O my soul.

O LORD my God, you are very great;
you are clothed with splendor and majesty.

2 He wraps himself in light as with a garment;
he stretches out the heavens like a tent

3 and lays the beams of his upper chambers on their
waters.

He makes the clouds his chariot
and rides on the wings of the wind.

4 He makes winds his messengers,
flames of fire his servants.

5 He set the earth on its foundations;
it can never be moved.

6 You covered it with the deep as with a garment;
the waters stood above the mountains.

7 But at your rebuke the waters fled,
at the sound of your thunder they took to flight;

8 they flowed over the mountains,
they went down into the valleys,
to the place you assigned for them.

9 You set a boundary they cannot cross;
never again will they cover the earth.

10 He makes springs pour water into the ravines;
it flows between the mountains.

11 They give water to all the beasts of the field;
the wild donkeys quench their thirst.

12 The birds of the air nest by the waters;
they sing among the branches.

13 He waters the mountains from his upper chambers;
       the earth is satisfied by the fruit of his work.
14 He makes grass grow for the cattle,
       and plants for man to cultivate—
       bringing forth food from the earth:
15 wine that gladdens the heart of man,
       oil to make his face shine,
       and bread that sustains his heart.
16 The trees of the LORD are well watered,
       the cedars of Lebanon that he planted.
17 There the birds make their nests;
       the stork has its home in the pine trees.
18 The high mountains belong to the wild goats;
       the crags are a refuge for the coneys.
19 The moon marks off the seasons,
       and the sun knows when to go down.
20 You bring darkness, it becomes night,
       and all the beasts of the forest prowl.
21 The lions roar for their prey
       and seek their food from God.
22 The sun rises, and they steal away;
       they return and lie down in their dens.
23 Then man goes out to his work,
       to his labor until evening.
24 How many are your works, O LORD!
       In wisdom you made them all;
       the earth is full of your creatures.
25 There is the sea, vast and spacious,
       teeming with creatures beyond number—
       living things both large and small.

26 There the ships go to and fro,
    and the leviathan, which you formed to frolic there.

27 These all look to you
    to give them their food at the proper time.

28 When you give it to them,
    they gather it up;
when you open your hand,
    they are satisfied with good things.

29 When you hide your face,
    they are terrified;
when you take away their breath,
    they die and return to the dust.

30 When you send your Spirit,
    they are created,
    and you renew the face of the earth.

31 May the glory of the LORD endure forever;
    may the LORD rejoice in his works—

32 he who looks at the earth, and it trembles,
    who touches the mountains, and they smoke.

33 I will sing to the LORD all my life;
    I will sing praise to my God as long as I live.

34 May my meditation be pleasing to him,
    as I rejoice in the LORD.

35 But may sinners vanish from the earth
    and the wicked be no more.

Praise the LORD, O my soul.

Praise the LORD.

William Wordsworth:

Composed a few miles above Tintern Abbey,
on revisiting the banks of the Wye during a tour.

July 13, 1798

FIVE years have past; five summers, with the length
Of five long winters! and again I hear
These waters, rolling from their mountain-springs
With a soft inland murmur.--Once again
Do I behold these steep and lofty cliffs,
That on a wild secluded scene impress
Thoughts of more deep seclusion; and connect
The landscape with the quiet of the sky.
The day is come when I again repose
Here, under this dark sycamore, and view   10
These plots of cottage-ground, these orchard-tufts,
Which at this season, with their unripe fruits,
Are clad in one green hue, and lose themselves
'Mid groves and copses. Once again I see
These hedge-rows, hardly hedge-rows, little lines
Of sportive wood run wild: these pastoral farms,
Green to the very door; and wreaths of smoke
Sent up, in silence, from among the trees!
With some uncertain notice, as might seem
Of vagrant dwellers in the houseless woods,   20
Or of some Hermit's cave, where by his fire
The Hermit sits alone.

These beauteous forms,
Through a long absence, have not been to me
As is a landscape to a blind man's eye:
But oft, in lonely rooms, and 'mid the din
Of towns and cities, I have owed to them
In hours of weariness, sensations sweet,
Felt in the blood, and felt along the heart;
And passing even into my purer mind,
With tranquil restoration:--feelings too   30
Of unremembered pleasure: such, perhaps,
As have no slight or trivial influence
On that best portion of a good man's life,
His little, nameless, unremembered, acts
Of kindness and of love. Nor less, I trust,
To them I may have owed another gift,
Of aspect more sublime; that blessed mood,
In which the burthen of the mystery,
In which the heavy and the weary weight
Of all this unintelligible world,   40
Is lightened:--that serene and blessed mood,
In which the affections gently lead us on,--
Until, the breath of this corporeal frame
And even the motion of our human blood
Almost suspended, we are laid asleep
In body, and become a living soul:
While with an eye made quiet by the power
Of harmony, and the deep power of joy,
We see into the life of things.

Genesis 2 leads us to God's Sabbath. God completed his work, rested, and blessed the Sabbath day. What does this mean? Was God tired? Did he need a vacation? No, his creative work came to a point of completion. God then took time to enjoy, even to savor what he had created. It is that God steps back to enjoy his creation—to be enriched by it. God blessed the Sabbath day. Imagine, God's taking time to enjoy or to rejoice over the work of his hands! To use a New York phrase, God was "jazzed" when he took it all in! This anticipates the pattern for man created in God's image. He is to work and create (in the limits of his finitude) and then to step back and enjoy the work he has done. Is he to have a different kind of day for fellowship with God and others—to reflect back on the work of his hands? Man's work is to bring joy to both himself and God. Sabbath here does not mean sleep, but joy and rejoicing. It is a reflection of God's own life.

The Sabbath day will become the special Covenant sign between God in Israel, a nation that is patterned after six days of work and one day of rest. In this sign, the Sabbath also expresses freedom in God. He provides and we are not under the bondage of economic pressures. When Israel was in Egypt, there was no liberty. Slaves can be called upon to work on any day and at any time. The Exodus freed our people from this bondage. It is therefore a memorial of the Exodus from Egypt. In the Jewish community, the coming of the Sabbath is celebrated as the coming of a bride. However, is not the bridal presence of the Sabbath really the extra degree of the presence of the Holy Spirit given on the Sabbath?

Bible Quotes on the Sabbath

Observe the Sabbath day by keeping it holy, as the Lord your God has commanded you. Six days you shall labor and do all your work, but the seventh day is a Sabbath to the LORD your God. On it you shall not do any work, neither you, nor you son or daughter, nor your manservant or maidservant, nor your ox, your donkey or any of your animals, nor the alien within your gaths, so that your manservant and maidservant may rest, as you do. Remember that you were slaves in Egypt and that the Lord your God brough you out of there with a mighty hand and an outstretched arm. Therefore the LORD your God has commanded you to observe the Sabbath day. (Deuteronomy 5:12-15)

Abraham Joshua Heschel on the Sabbath[5]

On the Sabbath, Heschel answers, humanity gets a sense of what the reward for "*teshuva*" is, namely, Paradise. But to appreciate the Sabbath requires "*teshuva*," it requires that humans "turn" away from their enslavement to things and money and open themselves up to another dimension, the dimension of spirit. In fact, to "welcome the Sabbath bride," to open onself to the Sabbath, is itself "*teshuva*," since it is a turning away from the weekaday world and an acceptance of God's dimension, an

---

5. Abraham Joshua Heschel, *The Sabbath, its Meaning for Man,* Farrar, Straus, and Giroux, 1951.

acknowledgement of God's sovereignty over all creation, and an acknowledgment that God awaits one the next instant if only one looks beyond the things in space that occupy one's time. The Sabbath is *Teshuva*, and it is also the reward for it. Both at once. The instant one perfoms the "turn," one gets the reward.

At this point, a reader who is steeped in classical philosophical ideas of God may ask how God, who is defined as self sufficient, can be enriched by something outside of himself. The question shows how far philosophical and theological thought moved from biblical thinking. That the everlasting God can be enriched by his creation seems hard to comprehend. However, there are so many texts that say that God takes pleasure in his people, that he is pleased with the incense that is burned before him, that our prayers can be as incense, and that God rejoices in his people. Any idea that God is not enriched by his creation, flies in the face of the whole witness of the Bible. Now it may be that God simply decided that he would create and be so enriched. Perhaps he did not have to be. However, it may also be argued that it is God's nature as love that he would be enriched by fellowship with human beings. The evidence of the Bible, that God is enriched by his people and by the creation, is overwhelming.

Chapter II:

Man In God's Image, Genesis 2

The creation of man is the apex of God's creative work. In Genesis one, we read that "God created man in his own image," but Genesis two gives us more detailed information concerning this creation. We read that God created man using the stuff of the earth for his body, but breathed into his nostrils the breath of life, and man became a living person (Genesis 2:7). Here we see an expansion of revelation for further understanding of the dominion mandate that arises out of being in God's image (Ch. 1). Adam was put in a wonderful garden planted by God with trees that are good for fruit, including the tree of the knowledge of good and evil and the tree of life. He was told to care for the garden, to cultivate it and to keep it. Herein we find that man was not first a hunter-gatherer. At this point he did not eat meat. He was a farmer, a cultivator of fruit trees.

The garden is paradise. This is important for understanding God's original intent. Nature is not to be left alone as self-sufficient. Rather, it is to be cultivated. In so doing, there is mutual blessing. Man creates from nature and makes it more wonderful, and nature blesses man with the fruit that is responsibly brought forth. Man is given the freedom to eat freely from the trees of the garden except from the tree of the knowledge of good and evil. We are not to think of nature in its raw state as perfect in a kind of natural eco-idolatry. To preserve in a natural state can be good and important; however, it is also good to create in and from nature. Thus, we see the rugged beauty of the wilderness as well as the great beauty of that which is humanly contrived. Norway reflects the first kind of beauty, Switzerland the second. However, which is more beautiful? Who can say? Both uses of nature bring wonderful blessing through the astonishing, almost painful, beauty that is present for us to enjoy. Man is not to worship nature, but the God behind nature. To again quote Abraham Heschel, "Earth is not our mother but our sister."

We should note that much of the natural order reflects an amazing symbiosis. Nothing is independent. Even very small and insignificant animals may have major effects on an ecosystem. Even microscopic life shows forth interdependence in a type of mutual blessing. All of creation shows this. Bees pollinate the flowers and bless plant life, but also receive that what they make, honey. Man takes care of the bees and is blessed with honey as well. We could continue and give multiple examples without limit. Man's caring for nature then requires that he take the interdependence of the ecosystem into account.

Man's dominion over the animal creation is developed in Genesis two. He brought the beasts and birds to man to see what he would call them (2:19,20). The animals would be named according to Adam's decision. Naming is connected both to understanding and to giving the animals their meaning. Naming is a prophetic action. It is through language that we see the world. As philosophers in the school of phenomenology in Europe have taught, language both discloses and hides the world. God creates the heavens and the earth through speaking. The actual way man sees the animals and understands them is through the language by which he names them. In part, Adam is bringing a creative new dimension of meaning through prophetic naming. This is part of his being created in God's image and ruling. Naming and distinguishing are necessary for stewarding nature. Here is really the foundation of the origin of science. Science begins in classification. Aristotle was known for his studies and classifications. Scientific progress also depends on useful classification.

Man learns to both cultivate according to what brings greater fruitfulness and to relate to animal creation though naming and discernment. Man and nature is interdependent for mutual blessing. Many cultures retain myths of man and animals having a greater degree of intimacy and communion. Indeed, fairy tales as well create situations of a deeper communion between man and the animal creation. This probably is a memory of the quality of the relationship between man and animal before the fall. Animals were not wild but related to man in a most friendly way. Redemption accomplishes the restoration of this relationship of mutual blessing as described in Isaiah 11 where children lead formerly wild animals and play with poisonous snakes.

Psalm 8

For the director of music. According to *gittith.*
A psalm of David.

1 O Lord, our Lord,
    how majestic is your name in all the earth!

You have set your glory
    above the heavens.
2 From the lips of children and infants
    you have ordained praise
because of your enemies,
    to silence the foe and the avenger.

3 When I consider your heavens,
    the work of your fingers,
the moon and the stars,
    which you have set in place,
4 what is man that you are mindful of him,
    the son of man that you care for him?
5 You made him a little lower than the heavenly beings
    and crowned him with glory and honor.

6 You made him ruler over the works of your hands;
    you put everything under his feet:
7 all flocks and herds,
    and the beasts of the field,
8 the birds of the air,
    and the fish of the sea,
    all that swim the paths of the seas.

9 O Lord, our Lord,
    how majestic is your name in all the earth! (NIV)

Isaiah 11:6-9

6   The wolf will live with the lamb,
        the leopard will lie down with the goat,
    the calf and the lion and the yearling together;
        and a little child will lead them.
7   The cow will feed with the bear,
        their young will lie down together,
        and the lion will eat straw like the ox.
8   The infant will play near the hole of the cobra,
        and the young child put his hand into the viper's nest.
9   They will neither harm nor destroy
        on all my holy mountain,
    for the earth will be full of the knowledge of the LORD
        as the waters cover the sea. (Isaiah 11:6-9, NIV)

Isaiah 65:17-25

7   "Behold, I will create
        new heavens and a new earth.
    The former things will not be remembered,
        nor will they come to mind.
18   But be glad and rejoice forever
        in what I will create,
    for I will create Jerusalem to be a delight
        and its people a joy.
19   I will rejoice over Jerusalem
        and take delight in my people;
    the sound of weeping and of crying
        will be heard in it no more.
20   "Never again will there be in it
        an infant who lives but a few days,

or an old man who does not live out his years;
he who dies at a hundred
will be thought a mere youth;
he who fails to reach a hundred
will be considered accursed.
21 They will build houses and dwell in them;
they will plant vineyards and eat their fruit.
22 No longer will they build houses and others live in them,
or plant and others eat.
For as the days of a tree,
so will be the days of my people;
my chosen ones will long enjoy
the works of their hands.
23 They will not toil in vain
or bear children doomed to misfortune;
for they will be a people blessed by the LORD,
they and their descendants with them.
24 Before they call I will answer;
while they are still speaking I will hear.
25 The wolf and the lamb will feed together,
and the lion will eat straw like the ox,
but dust will be the serpent's food.
They will neither harm nor destroy
on all my holy mountain,"
says the LORD. (NIV)

Despite Adam's enjoyment of the animals, he requires a connection and communication that is deeper. Adam discerns that there is a need for human fellowship. However, he is not aware of how this human fellowship will be attained. God therefore causes a deep sleep to fall upon Adam out of whose rib (as the earth material part) he creates a woman. She is to be his companion. Adam is greatly enriched in meeting Eve and proclaims a relationship of mutual blessing in interdependence. Each will give to the other.

I believe we need to read Adam's words as an exclamation and not just as a statement of fact. It is also prophetic and prescriptive. She is (and future marriages are to be) "bone of my bones and flesh of my flesh." Adam has headship over Eve before the fall as evidenced by Ephesians 5 and I Timothy 2:15. That he names the woman is an expression of this authority. However, it is an authority over one who is the deepest and most intimate companion. Indeed, we then read the proclamation, "A man shall leave his father and mother and cleave to his wife and they shall be one flesh." The ideal picture is monogamy—one man for one woman. Man and woman are interdependent for mutual blessing. This is so for their fellowship, the joy of their sexual relationship, and the bringing forth of children. The male/female distinction for mutual blessing is one of the greatest of all creation distinctions. It effects the human race constantly; it is not a distinction that is only significant for marriage. The blessing of this distinction in mutual interdependence is found in giving. *The whole order of the universe is based on love whereby one seeks to give to the other in compassionate indentification. To give is primary in every relationship; to receive is secondary.* With regard to man and woman, each gives first to the other and receives in return.

The Ephesians Analogy between Marriage and Yeshua and his People

[22] Wives, submit to your husbands as to the Lord. [23] For the husband is the head of the wife as Christ is the head of the church, his body, of which he is the Savior. [24] Now as the church submits to Christ, so also wives should submit to their husbands in everything.

[25] Husbands, love your wives, just as Christ loved the church and gave himself up for her [26] to make her holy, cleansing her by the washing with water through the word, [27] and to present her to himself as a radiant church, without stain or wrinkle or any other blemish, but holy and blameless. [28] In this same way, husbands ought to love their wives as their own bodies. He who loves his wife loves himself. [29] After all, no one ever hated his own body, but he feeds and cares for it, just as Christ does the church— [30] for we are members of his body. [31] "For this reason a man will leave his father and mother and be united to his wife, and the two will become one flesh." [32] This is a profound mystery—but I am talking about Christ and the church. [33] However, each one of you also must love his wife as he loves himself, and the wife must respect her husband. (Ephesians 5, NIV).

Elizabeth Barret Browning (1850)

How do I love thee? Let me count the ways.
I love thee to the depth and breadth and height
My soul can reach, when feeling out of sight
For the ends of Being and ideal Grace.
I love thee to the level of everyday's
Most quiet need, by sun and candlelight.
I love thee freely, as men might strive for Right;
I love thee purely, as they turn from Praise.
I love thee with the passion put to use
In my old griefs, and with my childhood's faith.
I love thee with a love I seemed to lose
With my lost saints,–I love thee with the breath,
Smiles, tears, of all my life!–and, if God choose,
I shall but love thee better after death.

The understanding of the original creation ideal for male and female in the human race is of paramount importance because it provides the foundation for understanding the effects of the fall and the meaning of the restoration of the creation. As we noted previously men and women are both created in the image of God. Women are no less valuable as persons than men. However, as biblical history develops, we see clearly that there are God-intended differences in roles. This is one of the great puzzles to westerners, especially at the turn of this century. We have lost the ability to distinguish between male and female.

Contemporary society interprets justice in terms of equality. Equality is understood in terms of sameness. Therefore, role distinctions between men and women are considered unjust. Biblically justice is only equality with regard to specifically defined dimensions in life. For example, men and women are equal before the law in crime and punishment. Both are equally valued by God. Both are given equal access to salvation and fellowship with God through the Messiah ("There is neither male or female ..." (Gal. 3:28)). Both are new creations in the New Covenant and seated with Him in heavenly places (I Cor. 5:17, Ephesians 2:5). Ultimately biblical justice seeks to restore God's order of righteousness. That order is not defined by equality. It is defined by each person and created thing fulfilling the order and purpose for which it was created to function in God's scheme of things. Sin, on the contrary, destroys that order. Sin seeks to dissolve God's distinctions for mutual blessing and produces a leveling. Nature and man are leveled in New Age philosophies, and nature is called god or part of god. Men and women are to be the same. Little girls and boys must play with both trucks and dolls to avoid forcing them into received cultural molds. There should be 50% women in all professions at all levels. According to the most radical feminists, it is considered more ideal that babies should be raised in incubators rather than a womb. This would be thought more just than that which is given by biology. There should be equality in both being elders in congregations as well as pastors and senior gift ministers (Eph. 4:25-5:2). This false definition of justice seeks to break down distinctions of gifting and calling whereby some will be wealthy and some of modest means, some will be leaders and some followers. Marxism expresses it in radical political, economic and social terms. Existentialism expresses it philosophically where it is taught that there is no creative essence given to men and women, but that we can choose to make ourselves according to whatever we desire in the most radical freedom. At any rate, we give all these examples to note that leveling as a false justice ideal permeates our society. We should be suspicious with regard to all radical leveling ideas.

I do want to say that gender distinctions are not easy to describe. There are people who believe that men and women are to be more equal both in roles in the larger society and government roles of leadership in the Body of Believers. They will point to other factors of complimentary gifting. There is a battle on these issues between those who call themselves complimentarians and those who are egalitarians. Some steer a middle course and think that men are to be the heads of their homes but that women can be heads of congregations. It is not my purpose to solve this debate here. I am a complimentarian who seeks the widest possible opportunity for women according to their gifts and talents. I do later note some of the best material that argues this.

The Bible does describe societies with significant role distinctions. Not all may be normative, but may be cultural. However, as biblical history develops we see a consistent description of leadership by tribal heads and heads of clans which is given to men. This is recognized by most as the patriarchal order of the Hebrew Scriptures. It is also reflected in almost all societies, primitive and civilized. Is this patriarchal order a product of God's creation order? Or is it a product of the fall and to be reversed through redemption? It becomes clear that at least some aspects of patriarchy are willed by God and are rooted in creation order. For example, Ephesians 5 clarifies that the husband is the head of his wife as Messiah is the head of the Church. We find in this passage that the distinction of roles between husbands and wives was designed from the beginning to be a reflection of the relationship of Messiah and the Church. I Timothy 2:15 points to a distinction whereby men are given the government of the Church as something rooted in the creation order. Man was created first to show priority in authority and government, and woman was taken out of man. In addition, Yeshua picks twelve men to be his disciples and Apostles as the foundational elders of the new community of faith. So also, eldership is given to men who prove themselves as heads of their homes in I Timothy 3 and Titus 1.

One of the difficulties in distinguishing men and women is that men and women have overlapping gifts and that the drawing of proper distinctions is difficult. We are in need of revelation to make the proper distinctions. Passages in the Bible show women in significant roles of ministry including Debroah in the book of Judges, Pricilla in the New Covenant, and others. The women were the first witnesses to the Resurrection. Yet no passage of Scripture calls upon the Body of Believers to appoint women to governmental eldership. I think the evidence for wide ministry opportunity is in the Bible, but there is no specific mention of ultimate governmental eldership.

Thus far, it is most important to note that God created man in his own image for mutual blessing. God desires that man would enjoy him and be blessed by him. God desires that he would be blessed by man's loving him and making of his creation something even more wonderful by applying his creative gifts to it. Nature is not fixed and final, but is a beautiful raw material for man to bring offerings back to God.

The great Russian Orthodox theologian Paval Florensky in *The Pillar and Ground of Truth*[1], saw that God's order is truth and beauty. Beauty is an objective manifestation of truth. In setting man and nature in mutual blessing and God and man in mutual blessing, both are enriched beyond description. God also enjoys his participation in the relationship between man and woman. Man and woman give praise to God in this relationship.

---

1. Pavel Florensky, *The Pillar and Ground of Truth,* Princeton University Press, Princeton, New Jersey, 1997.

Chapter III:

Man as Male and Female

God created two kinds of human beings. If he had desired all to play the same roles, would it not have been expected that he would have created one kind of human being, perhaps a biologically bisexual human being? In an age where justice is misunderstood as the equality of sameness, it is important to draw distinctions. Steve Clark, in his monumental book *Men and Women in Christ,*[1] does a fine job in pointing out distinctions, some of which are subtle. Clark uses sociological studies to enhance the biblical perspective.

Of course, because we are beings with physical senses, the first perception of distinctions is in the sensory realm. Man is generally larger and stronger than woman. This is biologically based in testosterone, ACTH and other genetic foundations. The famous Neo Orthodox theologian of the last century, Emil Brunner, pointed out that the very physical bodily differences between male and female lead to differences in psychological-self perceptions. This includes the idea of authority. Leadership, drive, and protection are innate to the men. Society can blunt

---

1. [8] Steve Clark, *Men and Women in Christ*, Servant Books, Ann Arbor, Michigan, 1980.

these instincts, but they are God given. Nurturing, nesting and following are more innate to women. However, this is not to say that each sex does not exhibit some of the characteristics of the other (or do not sometimes desire and legitimately exercise exceptional roles) but that there is more of a predominance of traits in one than the other. We see this even in childhood. Trying to get little boys to play domestic games with dolls and little girls to be interested in trucks, military games and more has largely failed. Just last week as I was writing this, the local newspaper reported that advertisers and television programmers were reverting to distinctions in shows, some geared to girls and some to boys.

To destroy the distinctions between the sexes is to lesson the attraction between the sexes that arises from the mystery of distinction and mutual blessing. George Gilder, in his monumental book *Men and Marriage*,[2] and Margie Gallagher, in her book *Enemies of Eros*,[3] both point out how detrimental the trend of over-equaliztion is for marriage and family. Guilder predicts an increase in homosexuality. Though there may be a genetic component for some homosexuality, the environment is still important in the view of many researchers. We find that role differentiation is universal in the history of cultures. Biblical culture is only one example. Patriarchy, namely men normally performing the roles of leadership in family, clan and tribe, predominates. Guilder points out that there has never been a prosperous matriarchal society. God calls Abraham and makes of him a great nation. A kingly line is established by David. The Messiah comes and chooses twelve male disciples. This is so

2. [9] George Gilder, *Men and Marriage,* Pelican, New Orleans, 1986.
3. [10] Margie Galliger, Enemies of Eros, Bonus Books, Chicago, 1989.

obvious and is recognized by most neutral observers. Only those who want to hold to the authority of the Bible but are already egalitarians think the biblical material is ambiguous. Scholars who are not believers in biblical authority see the implications as obvious and simply reject the patterns.

However, the roles given to men in priesthood, rulership, and family order do not imply that women are of lesser worth. Rather, women are given experiences of such depth of meaning that, from another perspective, it seems that women have been unfairly favored by God. This is contingent on the man fulfilling his role to be a blessing to woman. If he does so, she will be a great blessing to him. In the garden, Satan called for equality, for the man to usurp God, the woman to usurp man and God, and the man to abdicate responsibility to the woman. However, God calls us to find distinct roles for mutual blessing. In a biblical context, the man's role as primary family provider releases the woman to the fullness of nurture and relationships. Women are gifted in the intuitive and in the relational to a larger degree than men. For men, there must be great effort to attain the intimacy that is so natural to women. Intimacy is a high value in Scripture. In addition, women have the ability to bear and deliver children. This is an overwhelming source of intimacy with the nature of creation itself. To bear, deliver and nurse a baby is so deep and fulfilling that men can hardly begin to comprehend it. The man works or provides that the woman might fulfill this role with freedom. He partly enters into the experience, but can only vaguely grasp the emotional depth of the fulfillment. Yet, in mutual blessing, the man and the woman will both enjoy the children and all of the enrichment they bring into life.

We should also take note of the sexual relationship and its fulfillment. Society is most puzzled to find that the most sexually fulfilled people are in committed marriages.[4] Married religious people are more sexually fulfilled than secular people. There have been many surveys showing this. Something is wrong with the expectations of secular hedonism. Indeed, in the very sexual roles we see distinction for mutual blessing. The man enjoys pursuing; the woman being pursued. The women is stimulated by communication, caring, gentleness. The man is greatly fulfilled in giving this. The woman's response is more gradual in building and more gradually subsides after orgasm. The man therefore must accommodate the women in patience and continued love expression after the climax. The man is stimulated by sight, the woman by the tenderness of touch. However, these distinctions are not absolute but predominate. If the man is only lusting and not showing genuine love, he will not be blessed by the woman in return. The excitement of role reversal where the woman pursues and the man is receptive are exciting just because they are recognized as reversals of the normal roles. Both enjoy tenderness and gentleness. Both enjoy playful frolicking. However, there is a normal pattern that derives from sexual differentiation and which provides mutual blessing. The woman receives in a greater degree

---

4. Researchers at the University of Chicago seem to think so. Several years ago, when they released the results of the most "comprehensive and methodologically sound" sex survey ever conducted, they reported that religious women experience significantly higher levels of sexual satisfaction than non-religious women.

While this outcome caught some by surprise, the Chicago study was hardly the first to show a link between spirituality and sexuality. In fact, a 1940s Stanford University study, a 1970s Redbook magazine survey of 100,000 women and at least one other study from the early 1990s all found higher levels of sexual satisfaction among women who attend religious services.

and the man gives in a greater degree. Our very physiology shows this to be so. It is in mutual differences that we find the mutual blessing of the sexual relationship of our total love and acceptance of the other. In a good marriage, both are committed and live out a pattern of blessing the other. This is not only in the sexual realm, but in all regards. We could also note that the sexual relationship of the man and the woman is physically akin to the Temple. We can see the dimensions of outer court, inner court and most holy place in the physical uncovering, especially in the case of the woman. Just as only the high priest was to enter the most holy place, so only the husband enters the holy place of the physical love of his wife. We see such thoughts in the understanding of the Temple by scholars Margaret Barker and Mary Douglas.

Let us note how Scripture brings out this differentiation in both Genesis and the New Covenant Scriptures. In Genesis, man is created first and woman is created as his helper. Yes, she is a partner; she is created for fellowship. She is not a slave. However, it is clearly reflected throughout the Scriptures that man is in leadership in the marriage and family. This is even further clarified in Ephesians 5. Here we find that male leadership is not a product of the fall. Male abuse is such a product. The redemptive picture of Ephesians 5 is that marriage was meant to be a microcosmic picture of a macrocosmic reality. The man is parallel to the Messiah. He is to love his wife as the Messiah loves the congregation and lay his life down for her. He is to encourage her by the Word of God, which is called the washing by the Word. The wife is to submit to her husband in everything, as the Congregation is to submit to Yeshua. We see in Scripture that the man is given the greater responsibility for leadership and provision for the family. He may enlist the wife to help in this responsibility (Prov. 31). We read in addition, "Her husband can trust her, and she will greatly enrich his life. She will not hinder him, but help in all her life." Myles Monroe points out that the man is called to bring out the best in his wife and family.[5] His goal is to enable them to fulfill their destinies according to their gifts and callings. Because the wife has her own distinct callings and gifts, the husband does not just seek her service for his own sake, but serves here and fosters the fulfillment of her calling. This is parallel to Yeshua and his people. Just as the Messiah and his Congregation are not equal in authority and leadership, so is the case with the husband and wife. In addition, other passages such as I Peter 3:1-6 speak of the wife's obeying her husband. She is called to respect her husband (Eph. 5:33). In such a marriage, there is great mutual blessing. I Peter 3:1-7 and Ephesians 5: 21-33 bear quoting in full.

Wives and Husbands

[22] Wives, submit to your husbands as to the Lord. [23] For the husband is the head of the wife as Christ is the head of the church, his body, of which he is the Savior. [24] Now as the church submits to Christ, so also wives should submit to their husbands in everything.

[25] Husbands, love your wives, just as Christ loved the church and gave himself up for her [26] to make her holy, cleansing her by the washing with water

---

5. [12] Myles Monroe, the famous mega church pastor from Nassau, Behammas, in oral lectures in 1994, Mid East Leadership Conference, Gettysburg, Pennsylvania.

through the word, [27] and to present her to himself as a radiant church, without stain or wrinkle or any other blemish, but holy and blameless. [28] In this same way, husbands ought to love their wives as their own bodies. He who loves his wife loves himself. [29] After all, no one ever hated his own body, but he feeds and cares for it, just as Christ does the church— [30] for we are members of his body. [31] "For this reason a man will leave his father and mother and be united to his wife, and the two will become one flesh." [32] This is a profound mystery—but I am talking about Christ and the church. [33] However, each one of you also must love his wife as he loves himself, and the wife must respect her husband. [6] (NIV)

Let us give some examples of this mutuality. The husband is to appreciate the greater intuitive capacity of his wife and to benefit from it. Indeed, if he listens to his wife, he will be saved from many pitfalls. Reservations in her spirit are an important factor in decision-making. One executive testified that he would never hire key staff unless they first met his wife and she had no major intuitive concerns. On the other hand, the wife is to learn to appreciate the analytical conservatism of her husband. This prevents rash decisions. Of course, these are ideals. Self-centeredness and immaturity break down the design of how we were meant to function.

In addition, the wife is able to bear and give birth to children. She gives primary nurturing to young children,

---

6. *The Holy Bible: New International Version.* 1996 (electronic ed.) (Eph 5:21–33). Grand Rapids, MI: Zondervan.

especially during the nursing period. The husband delights in observing his wife's nurturing ability and develops greater ability himself through his wife's example. However, the husband will usually be more capable in training older children, especially boys, out of his leadership capacities. Men are often better with older children. Their participation in the lives of their children differs.

I do not want the reader to think that I am speaking of enforcing *rigid limitations* for what men and women may do. Some women have unique gifts for business (Prov. 31) or leadership (Margaret Thatcher). On the other hand, it is a tragic mistake for society to force women and men into conformity to parity in roles that neither biology nor God's creation order supports. The fact of differentiation is resisted by many of today's egalitarians, but even secular writers see that there are differences between the sexes. This is given witness by the popular book by psychologist John Gray *Men Are From Mars, Women are from Venus*.[7]

When the man and the woman learn to appreciate their distinctiveness, and the roles that flow out of such distinctions as clarified by the revelation of Scripture, there is wonderful mutual blessing. The context of love where each seeks to outdo the other in serving produces joy. The man serves the wife as Messiah, voluntarily and continually laying down his life. The wife seeks to please the husband in respect, submission and support. He keeps the image of Yeshua in his vision; she keeps the image of his bride-congregation in mind. The levels of intimacy and joy in the relationship of marriage are

---

7. [14] John Gray, *Men are from Mars and Women from Venus*, New York, Harper Collins, 1992.

beyond description. However, even those not married can, in the context of congregation and society, be greatly enriched by relationships between men and women and the different qualities they bring into varieties of situations. Because not every man and every woman fit the general pattern of distinct qualities, and because discerning these distinctions without biblical revelation is difficult, some have come to doubt these distinctions. We reject and doubt them at our peril.

A few other Scriptures should be given to support this understanding. One is I Peter 3:6 where we read of the image of Sarah who was humble and faithful and called Abraham her Lord (master). In addition, I Corinthians 12-14 gives instruction for men and women in operating in the gifts of the Spirit. Women are not to exercise gifts in such a way that they would be exercising authority over men. So Paul states that he does not permit a woman to exercise authority over men. Teaching in the ancient world was in a context of discipling: a father to son type of relationship. Where public teaching does not imply such a relationship, I believe there is much greater flexibility. Women are not to father-disciple men (I Tim 2:11-15). In addition, we see in I Timothy 3 that only men by virtue of the fact that they have proven good leadership in their families are described as being called to be the elders in the government of congregations. Does this preclude singles or other exceptions? Perhaps not, but this is the general pattern set forth. In conclusion, Scripture does support role differentiation based on God's order of creation. It does also allow for some crossover as in Deborah, but does also uphold the general pattern.

We can see that this relationship of marriage is one of the greatest blessings of mutual differentiation. Both men and women are fully human beings created in the image of God. Both are heirs of eternal life. Yet there is such a difference. Since leadership in congregational life is largely family-based, it is largely patriarchal. However, the New Covenant Scriptures break with their contemporary culture in giving women wide rules of opportunity for the public use of their gifts if exercised under elders. In general, male and female differences, down to the very hormones and the genetics of every cell, will be naturally expressed in general patterns of male motivation and drive and female nurturing in imparting to the congregation. Each can manifest some of the aspects of the other, but the dominant traits are still different. Again, one of the great errors of contemporary thinking is that having lost God, and having lost a sense of worth in him, we seek to find worth by leveling all into sameness to prevent jealousy or to seek a false definition of justice. This destroys mutual blessing. I do not need to be blessed by what is the duplicate of me. Justice is not sameness, but that order which best enables all to fulfill their roles, gifts, callings and destinies.

Let us note that all of these ideals are only attained through identification with his crucifixion where we die to selfishness in order to serve the other. Olivier Claimont states in the Orthodox Christian Catechism, *The Living God*[8]:

> The holy martyrs-- 'who fought the good fight and received your crowns'—are asked to help the newlyweds wage a good fight also so that in the end they too may attain a crown of glory. Married life is not easy. It involves a hard struggle, a total rejection

---

8. [15] Olivier Clement, *Living God, A Catechism for the Christian Faith,* Crestwood, New York, St. Vladimir's Seminary Press 1989.

of egotism, and the joyful acceptance of the Cross. It is an ascetic exercise through which one dies to oneself so that each may live for the other. 'O Lord our God ... let that gladness come upon us which the blessed Helen had when she found the precious Cross.' We are not ironical in comparing marriage to a holy martyrdom."

On Marriage

1 How beautiful you are, my darling!
   Oh, how beautiful!
   Your eyes behind your veil are doves.
   Your hair is like a flock of goats
      descending from Mount Gilead.
2 Your teeth are like a flock of sheep just shorn,
      coming up from the washing.
   Each has its twin;
      not one of them is alone.
3 Your lips are like a scarlet ribbon;
      your mouth is lovely.
   Your temples behind your veil
      are like the halves of a pomegranate.
4 Your neck is like the tower of David,
      built with elegance;
   on it hang a thousand shields,
      all of them shields of warriors.
5 Your two breasts are like two fawns,
      like twin fawns of a gazelle
      that browse among the lilies.

6 Until the day breaks
     and the shadows flee,
   I will go to the mountain of myrrh
     and to the hill of incense.
7 All beautiful you are, my darling;
     there is no flaw in you.

8 Come with me from Lebanon, my bride,
     come with me from Lebanon.
   Descend from the crest of Amana,
     from the top of Senir, the summit of Hermon,
   from the lions' dens
     and the mountain haunts of the leopards.
9 You have stolen my heart, my sister, my bride;
     you have stolen my heart
   with one glance of your eyes,
     with one jewel of your necklace.
10 How delightful is your love, my sister, my bride!
     How much more pleasing is your love than wine,
     and the fragrance of your perfume than any spice!
11 Your lips drop sweetness as the honeycomb, my bride;
     milk and honey are under your tongue.
     The fragrance of your garments is like that of
       Lebanon.
12 You are a garden locked up, my sister, my bride;
     you are a spring enclosed, a sealed fountain.
13 Your plants are an orchard of pomegranates
     with choice fruits,
     with henna and nard,
14   nard and saffron,

calamus and cinnamon,
with every kind of incense tree,
with myrrh and aloes
and all the finest spices.
15 You are a garden fountain,
a well of flowing water
streaming down from Lebanon.

(NIV: *Song of Songs*)

Chapter IV:

Israel and The Nations

Man was created by God for mutual blessing. However, in the fall, man sought to be equal to God, even the same as God, and thus destroyed the mutual blessing relationship. Man was created for submitted partnership with God—to rule wisely over the creation. Biblical history, called by the late Protestant French theologian Oscar Cullman "salvation history," is the story of God's work to restore man to submitted partnership. Only in such a partnership of mutual blessing can man be fulfilled. Because man made the choice of autonomy from God, by partaking of the fruit of the tree of the knowledge of good and evil, man must seek to be restored to his right order.

The tree of the knowledge of good and evil has been variously interpreted. One of the finest treatments is Rick Joyner's *There Were Two Trees in the Garden.*[1] The choice of the wrong tree was a choice to live by reason and experience rather than by the revelation of God. What a terrible choice! It is not that we were not to have reason or experience, but we were to

---

1. [16] Rick Joyner, *There Were Two Trees in the Garden*, Morningstar Publications, Charlotte, North Carolina, 1986.

enjoy these gifts within their limits. The tree of the knowledge of good and evil represents a proud claim that we can figure it out for ourselves. However, we cannot reason about what we do not see; revelation and obedience come first. Like teenagers seeking their independence, man said something like, "How can I know it is bad if I have not tried it?" Human reason and experience cannot lead us to the ultimate truths without which we cannot find fulfillment. In sin, we are blinded, and our reasoning is darkened. Claiming to be wise we become fools. We can see the choice for autonomy in our own recent cultural history. Why did we live in the 1950s without locking our doors, and without needing as many controls on guns and other restrictions on freedom? It was because the people of that time embraced their dependence on God. The moral foundation of our society in God was taken seriously. Children were trained in this foundation. There was security. There was low crime, good schools, intact families, and a sense of living within a fulfilling order. The ten commandments permeated society as seen in the movie *The Ten Commandments*. When autonomy from God was chosen, decline was inevitable. This includes a loss character in the people and a need for more external controls. This repeats the choice and the consequences of Adam and Eve.

The fallen state of Adam and Eve was passed on to their children. Their descendent Noah gave birth to the children who will become nations or peoples. The origin of nations in Genesis 9 and 10 leads us into the story of Abraham (Genesis 12) whose grandson, Jacob, gave birth to the fathers of the tribes of Israel. The story of Israel is the story of God's work to win the nations back to himself. First, God needed to find a man who was wholly given to the purposes of God. In Abraham, he found one such man. Could any other be considered greater? Abraham not only obeyed in leaving his family, but developed an unparalleled ability to hear the voice of God. He was a prophet, priest and king. The purpose of Abraham and his descendants, the children of Israel, was to bring blessing to all of the nations (Gen. 12:3). It was to reverse the fall. A man had to come to God in such a way that the course of history would be changed—so that history would move toward the full redemption of the human race.

The ultimate test of Abraham was the command to sacrifice Isaac. God called Isaac Abraham's only son even though Abraham had a son by the name of Ishmael. Isaac, not Ishmael, was God's son of promise. For God's covenant purposes of redemption, Isaac was the only son of the promise. The covenant between God and Abraham was a covenant of mutual blessing that was to bring blessing to the world. God called Abraham as the high priest of the human race to sacrifice his son. This was the amazing level of friendship that Abraham developed with God. Here was the great test; would Abraham now follow the path of the tree of the knowledge of good and evil and disobey this command? Human reason would say that God's orders must be disobeyed, for it would thwart the covenant promise that blessing to the nations would come through Isaac. Furthermore, how could Abraham give his own son? The New Covenant Scriptures see the answer in Abraham's faith, that God could raise Isaac from the dead. The sacrifice of Isaac is amazingly parallel to the sacrifice of Yeshua. Both are the only sons of their fathers. Both are offered as a sacrifice. Both are received back from the dead (one symbolically, the other literally). The sacrifice of Isaac is the great intercessory priestly act for the whole human race that would lead to the coming of the Messiah to die for the sins of the world. Abraham shows submitted partnership in obedience to revelation instead of asserting his autonomy. As high priest he representatively offers the human race back to God in submitted partnership. My sense is that without such a covenant act on a man's part, the Messiah would not have come to die and be raised from the dead for our sins. The blessing that will come from Israel to the nations, anticipated in the covenant with Abraham, is amazing. The embrace of One Creator God, the moral standards of the law, civil laws standards, and ultimately the Messiah are some of the amazing blessings to the world from Israel. The whole Bible, Genesis to Revelation, is a Jewish product!

After the Exodus, Israel's whole life was organized to bring blessing to the nations. The sacrificial system participated in the meaning of the death of Isaac and called forth the coming of the Messiah to die for the sins of the world. The whole nation was organized around the Tabernacle and later the Temple. It was for the world. The nation was organized to support the Temple in tithes, bringing offerings, and giving the priests an inheritance. Cohanim (priests), Levites, and the ordinary Israelites were arranged according to different responsibilities for mutual enrichment or blessing. The Cohanim performed the service and sacrifice for all Israel and for the nations. The nation of Israel supplied the Cohanim with their needs. The Levites served the Cohanim and were provided for by the nation of Israel as well. Every sacrifice participated in the meaning of the sacrifice of Isaac and called for the coming of the Messiah as God's great gift of sacrifice and life for the world. This included the offerings offered corporately for Israel daily, on the Sabbath and on the Feasts. It included the Yom Kippur Sacrifice for Israel once a year. This included the Passover offering for each family. I also believe that the sacrifices preserved the world in existence until the Messiah would come and die. In the movie *Ben Hur*, we have the wonderful picture of the blood of Yeshua running into the streams of water and permeating the whole world. The feast of Sukkot (Tabernacles) in the Fall especially has the nations in view. Numbers describes 70 bulls offered. The ancient rabbis tell us that 70 is the number of the nations and that these sacrifices were for the sins of the world.

Though Israel is to be kept separate from the nations, she is to be visible to the nations. Her land is on the trade routes connecting three continents (Europe, Asia and Africa). God seeks to establish a way of life that is to be a witness. First is the witness of Israel's origins. She is brought forth as a nation of slaves and is delivered from Egypt. As a nation of priests or mediators for the nations, Israel undergoes suffering, for God sees the nature of life under the fall as slavery. Israel's slavery is intercessory identification. Most nations have been subdued by the more powerful and enslaved at various levels. God desires that all nations be brought out of bondage into a promised land. The celebration of Passover still testifies to this truth. It is an intercessory celebration releasing power toward the goal of the liberation of all the nations.

Ideally, the nations are to see that the quality of life in Israel is far superior to life anywhere else. Obedience to God brings this blessing. It is a most humane life where the lowliest can enjoy the Sabbath, where there is provision for the poor and where the courts are just for all people. Work is not to be a dominating slavery to Israelites. Idolatry is rejected, and the worship of the one true God established. In this context, the nations are to see that life under God's rule is best. Israel then demonstrates the abundant provision of God and the power of God. In her times of faithfulness, she is invincible and needs to enter no foreign alliances. She must not share the gods of the nations, as sharing is part of alliance making. She is to walk by faith in God. The Covenant of Abraham is a faith covenant. It required Abraham to leave his people and to trust in the provision of God. The Covenant through Moses is a faith covenant as well which applies the Abrahamic Covenant for that time. Parallel to Abraham, Israel is to trust God to protect them and to provide without resorting to fleshy means of self-protection. Keeping the Sabbath and Feasts was required, as well as trusting God even though many days would be free of work. In the same way, the forgiveness of debt and letting land lay fallow in the seventh year (sabbatical) and the Jubile year (the 50th) required faith. As Thomas McComiskey notes, the Mosaic Covenant was an administration of the Abrahamic Covenant for that time. In both covenants, obedience is a response of faith and love.[2]

What blessing came to the world through Israel! It is beyond adequate description. Israel preserved the Scriptures that became a key pillar of much of the World. The doctrines of man being made in the image of God, of the Law of God and of God's redemptive love for all peoples are the primary

---

2. Thomas McComiskey, *Covenants of Promise,* Baker Books, Grand Rapids, Michigan, 1985.

civilizing themes of world history. No other worldview leads to such humane progress. Yes, it is hard for man to get it; he does not live up to it. However, to the extent that the biblical revelation holds sway, civilization progresses. This is true of the positive dimensions of Islam as well, which go back to the Bible. Ethical monotheism is the great contribution of blessing from Israel to the world. Yes, Israel often failed, but she succeeded enough to bring this great blessing to the nations.

The Church is an institution created by God to also bring blessing to the nations. Its role is parallel to Israel's but also distinguishable. The Church for all nations and of all nations was given birth in the Temple when the Spirit fell at Pentecost. We should see that the context of the 120 meeting was not in the upper room, but in the Temple for the feast of Pentecost (Shavuot). The Temple Mount is such a place of gathering, which explains why thousands were easily able to assemble. In addition, it explains the immersions of thousands of new followers of Yeshua, for ample numbers of immersion pools were built at the entrances to the Temple to accommodate many people. The New Temple, whom we are, was birthed in the ancient Temple where the Glory previously came in the days of Solomon, where Abraham sacrificed Isaac! The Gospel was spread by faithful Jews to the Gentiles. Again, Israel brings blessing to the nations. We should also note that most New Covenant congregations from the mission of Barnabas and Paul and after with Paul and Silas, were birthed from the Synagogue.

How much more has Israel blessed the nations? From Israel comes the seven day week and the idea of a day off (a Sabbath). From Israel comes humane working laws. Jewish people continue to make amazing contributions for the blessing of the world in science, art, music, entertainment, business and much more. Yes, some Jewish people who have turned from God are a negative influence, but they have also contributed to the greatest positive influence upon the world

However, God's order is mutual blessing. It cannot be that Israel will bless the nations and not be blessed in return. There is a special relationship of Jew and Gentile in the One New Man called the Body of the Messiah which is a foreshadowing of the mutual blessing between Israel and the nations. Israel and the nations will be one under the rule of the Messiah. So in a foreshadowing way, Israel and the nations are within the Body of the Messiah. The Body of the Messiah is both the saved remnant of Israel and the saved remnant of the nations. However, the greater number by far is from the nations. It is most amazing that Romans 11 shows that this Body of the Messiah, and especially the Gentile followers of Yeshua, are to bring blessing to Israel. So in Romans 11, the Gentiles especially are charged with a priesthood of love and mercy to the Jewish nation. Paul says, "I am speaking to you Gentiles, inasmuch as I am an apostle to the Gentiles. I magnify my service if by any means I may provoke to jealousy those of my fellow Israelites and save some of them" (Rom. 11:14, my translation). How do we provoke Israel to jealousy, that is to be desirous of joining our faith in the Messiah Yeshua? To magnify our service, is to magnify the supernatural loving work of the Holy Spirit, to demonstrate that God is real and with us. In Romans 11:31, we see that we are to show mercy to the Jewish people. For this nation brought the Gentiles the Word of God, the Messiah, and the Good News. Mercy includes prayer-intercession, deeds of love, and a tactful witness to the truth. This can only be done if Gentiles show that they appreciate the good things about the Jewish people and their heritage. Therefore, God has established that the priesthood of the Jewish people and the priesthood of the Gentiles in the Church are complimentary. Without the Jewish priesthood fulfilling its role of witness to the nations in the last days and inviting Yeshua to rule all nations, we will not see the Kingdom of God come in fullness. Without the role of the Gentile priesthood, Israel will not come to see the truth and fulfill its role. So God has arranged things for mutual humility whereby both Jew and Gentile in the Messiah will honor and acknowledge the other with thanksgiving, "But for you I never would have made it."

In the Age to Come, Israel and the nations will bring blessing to each other. We have already noted from Isaiah 27:6 that Israel will "bud and blossom and blossom and fill the whole world with fruit" (NIV). However, all of the nations will bring their distinctive wealth to Israel as well (Isaiah 61:11). This is similar to the picture we see in Revelation 21:24 where all the nations bring their splendor into the New Jerusalem. We must not think of riches in a carnal and simplistic way. Rather, they bring their gifts and creativity to enrich the life of Israel and vice versa. Every nation brings its cultural enrichment into the New Jerusalem. Each culture is a distinctive corporate personality. It is shared in relationships of love and mutual blessing. The one who has pours out for the other to receive. Israel as the chief of the nations serves the other nations. The saved from this age rules as the bride of the Messiah and blesses and enriches Israel and the nations. These pictures are certainly beyond what we can literally comprehend.

This leads us to understand that each nation is uniquely valuable and has gifts for the blessing of humanity. The tower of Babel was the place of separating nations and languages. It was a punishment and a discipline for humanity. Humanity would not be in unity. However, behind the language separation was a blessing. Every language group has its unique angles for seeing. Its unique beauties, art, music, and technology will enrich humanity forever. In addition, part of the identity and personality of each person is formed by his culture. Beyond this, God's life is enriched by the corporate nations as well.

God does not only see people on an individual plane, but in a corporate way. Each nation, tribe and people is a corporate man, and the whole of humanity is a corporate man. At Pentecost, the languages are spoken supernaturally so that all can hear the Gospel. Humanity is unified again. Isn't it interesting that at Pentecost the nations did not all understand one language, instead the apostles spoke many languages? Is it possible that in the future, we will understand multiple languages? So there is blessing from nation to nation and from God to each nation and each nation to God, mutual enrichment forever.

We should note that life after the fall for the redeemed is largely a life of intercession. It is lived for the sake of the redemption of others. This is in direct prayer and in indirect means of intercession. The reward of the intercessor is bringing children to birth and maturity which will be to our enrichment forever. So Paul says that his spiritual children are his crown of rejoicing, his reward. Those who have been redeemed return gratitude to the intercessors and are blessed with the gift of salvation and maturity which comes through the prayers of others. Because man is over the natural order, the redemption of humankind and the natural order comes through the spread of the Good News by intercession and witness.

Blessing to Come to Israel and From Israel

Psalm 105, God's Covenant with Israel

⁶ Remember what he has done, you children of his servant
    Abraham.
    Remember it, you people of Jacob, God's chosen ones.
⁷ He is the LORD our God.
    He judges the whole earth.
⁸ He will keep his covenant forever.
    He will keep his promise for all time to come.
⁹ He will keep the covenant he made with Abraham.
    He will keep the oath he took when he made his promise
    to Isaac.
¹⁰ He made it stand as a law for Jacob.
    He made it stand as a covenant for Israel. It will last forever.
¹¹ He said, "I will give you the land of Canaan.
    It will belong to you (NIV)

From Robert Browning, "Holy Cross Day" (1855)

XIII

"The Lord will have mercy on Jacob yet,
And again in his border see Israel set.
When Judah beholds Jerusalem,
The stranger-seed shall be joined to them:
To Jacob's House shall the Gentiles cleave.
So the Prophet saith and his sons believe.

XIV

"Ay, the children of the chosen race
Shall carry and bring them to their place: In the land of the
Lord shall lead the same
Bondsmen and handmaids. Who shall blame,
When the slaves enslave, the oppressed ones o'er
The oppressor triumph for evermore?

John Milton from "Paradise Regained" (1671)

Yet at length, time to himself best known,
Remembering Abraham, bu some wondrous
May bring them back repentant and sincere,
And at their passing cleave the Assyrian Flood,
While to their native land with joy they haste,
As the Red Sea and Jordan once He cleft,
When to the Promised Land their fathers pass'd
To his due time and providence I leave them.

Chapter V:

Blessing and
Orders of Authority

Humanity rebels against God's orders of authority. However, understanding God's orders of authority and submitting to them will lead us into mutual enrichment.

All legitimate authority comes from God who is the ultimate authority over the universe because he is the creator of all things (Romans 13). While God gives man freedom to rebel against his authority, man can only find his fulfillment in submission to God. God gives us love, security, inspiration, life, gifts, anointing, creativity and more. He has provided us with all the good gifts of human relationships. He has provided us with all of the blessings of nature. Every good work of man, every great work of art and every great scientific advance are accomplished only with the aid of God. Indeed, we can say that a person creates something wonderful. We can give honor to the person who does the work. However, it is really a co-work with God. All good human works are therefore to the glory of God.

Submission to God as authority does not destroy our creativity but sets the boundaries wherein this freedom can flourish. This submission is first submission to God whereby we seek "To love Him with all our heart, soul, mind and strength" (Deut. 6:4, Mark 12). Our relationship with him is first and foremost. Then we submit to his written Word. His Word gives us the guidelines for fulfillment and mutual blessing. The creativity of our sexuality is fulfilled in monogamous heterosexual marriage. We are stewards of the earth and are to protect the environment that nature might bless us. We develop the means of provision and wealth creation in a context of generosity toward others. Honest labor and creativity is the rule of Torah. God is therefore behind all of the blessings that are received in proper relationships in all spheres of life.

This enables us to understand the nature of justice. Biblical justice is the establishing of God's order of righteousness. Justice in itself does not mean equality, except as qualified by Scripture. We are equally created in the image of God and are of equal worth before God as human beings. With regard to violating God's law, there is to be equality before the courts. God's order of righteousness is simply the order that enables every person to fulfill their callings and destinies that fits their God given gifts and abilities. It is also an order where every family, tribe and nation fulfills its destiny and life according to the application of God's Torah (God's pattern of relationship) for them. This is also expressed in cultural and artistic varieties in various peoples.

God's Order of Authority for Marriage

We have spoken of this before in the context of male and female in creation. Here, we want to again summarize with regard to the issue of authority spheres. The relationship between husband and wife is established in the earliest chapters of Genesis. In Genesis, we see that Adam is created first, and next Eve is created and called his helper. This helper role, though implying Adam's higher authority, does not imply his greater worth. Eve is given the privilege of bearing and nursing children. The Scripture proclaims a love relationship as the center of marriage for "a man shall leave his father and mother and cleave unto his wife and the two shall become one flesh" (Genesis 2:24). Adam's exclamation surely reflects enthusiasm; for Eve is "the bone of my bones and the flesh of my flesh" (Genesis 2:23). Though the fall perverts this relationship and other relationships to authority. In this case, a man may dominate and abuse the woman and the woman may desire and manipulate. There is a restoration in the New Covenant. The true nature of man's authority and the woman's submission is best put forward in Ephesians 5:

> [22] Wives, submit to your husbands as to the Lord. [23] For the husband is the head of the wife as Christ is the head of the church, his body, of which he is the Savior. [24] Now as the church submits to Christ, so also wives should submit to their husbands in everything.

> [25] Husbands, love your wives, just as Christ loved the church and gave himself up for her [26] to make her holy, cleansing her by the washing with water through the word, [27] and to present her to himself as a radiant church, without stain or wrinkle or any other blemish, but holy and blameless. [28] In this same way, husbands ought to love their wives as their own

bodies. He who loves his wife loves himself. [29] After all, no one ever hated his own body, but he feeds and cares for it, just as Christ does the church— [30] for we are members of his body. [31] "For this reason a man will leave his father and mother and be united to his wife, and the two will become one flesh." [32] This is a profound mystery—but I am talking about Christ and the church. [33] However, each one of you also must love his wife as he loves himself, and the wife must respect her husband. (NIV)

The relationship between husband and wife is said to be a microcosmic reflection of the relationship between the Messiah and his congregation. So the analogy becomes the pattern for understanding authority and submission. The husband is to love his wife as the Messiah loves his bride—the Church (Kehilah-corporate Congregation). He lays down his life for his bride, so the husband is to lay down his life for his wife. As the Messiah washes his bride with the water of the Word, so the husband is to encourage his wife by the Word of God. She becomes perfected in a context of acceptance and love. Even so the corporate Congregation of Yeshua becomes a glorious bride without spot or wrinkle.

The wife is told to submit to her husband as the corporate congregation submits to the Messiah. The husband is the overseer of the family. He seeks to hear the wisdom of his wife, and to see a consensus of agreement with his wife, yet the ultimate decision of leadership is with the husband. In addition, there are many other Scriptures that show the distinction intended by God between husband and wife. Today, our society seeks a sameness of roles, but Scripture again and again affirms the husband's overall authority over his wife and family. So in Peter 3:1 ff we read these words:

> In the same way, you wives, be submissive to your own husbands so that even if any of them are disobedient to the word, they may be won without a word by the behavior of their wives, as they observe your chaste and respectful behavior. ... So also the holy women also who hoped in God, used to adorn themselves, being submissive to their own husbands. Thus Sarah obeyed Abraham, calling him lord, and you have become her children if you do what is right without being frightened by any fear. (NIV)

Note the unbelieving husband as such is never told to be submitted to his wife. In addition, the husband's leadership quality over his wife and family in I Timothy 3 is one of the key qualifications for eldership, which is government in the congregation. The husband is in governmental headship in the family. The husband and wife put each other first and have a loving and serving heart toward one another. The wife respects the authority of her husband. They serve in a different consciousness. The husband has the model of the Messiah who lays down his life for the one over whom he has authority. The wife has in mind the bride of the Messiah who is submitted to the Word of the Messiah. Such a marriage is blissful. It is not difficult for a godly woman to submit to a godly, loving husband who is like the Messiah, though she is called to submit even if her husband is not like Yeshua. Even so the husband is required to lay down his life for a wife who has not learned the grace of submission.

When we look more closely, we see that the is a purpose for the differences between the genders. In general man's greater physical strength reflects his responsibility and authority. The wife's ability to bear and nurse children is a profound difference from the man. If she does not have children, other aspects of her femininity are still a significant complimentary difference. Even some tasks, the man's strength enables him to do harder physical work for the sake of the home. His tendency is toward logical analysis, though this difference is not universal, but a tendency. The woman is more naturally intuitive and relational. Each is called to learn from the gifts of the other. It is the consensus of husband and wife that bring a balanced safety in decision making when both are loving and godly. They each see in part and need the other to see more holistically. God has made us interdependent. The husband has in his heart and very constitution to be the primary one responsible for material provision, but may organize the family to help in this task. The husband is given greater responsibility to protect his family from crime and other dangers. At the same time, husband and wife share authority over children.

The greatness of the mutual enrichment of husband and wife is beyond words. Who can adequately describe the blessing of mutual enrichment in expressing our love in the sexual relationship of marriage? Who can recount the fullness of joy in that deep knowing of the other in the realm of the soul where there is a sense of great agreement as well as complimentary dimensions? The other intrigues us forever, so different and so alike. Upon reflection their thoughts, their communications in word and gesture and their kind caress can amaze us. That such a relationship can exist is proof of the goodness of God.

The husband is never called to suppress his wife, but to provide a context of love and appreciation for her to fulfill her gifts and calling. In addition, she supports him in his calling. Such differentiation between male and female does preclude each from some roles. However, we should not think that only the traditional roles of western society are open to husbands or wives. Both may be in the business and professional world. Both may be in politics and teaching. Scripture provides boundaries for men and women, but within those boundaries, there are vast possibilities for men and women in serving the Kingdom in various careers. It is only necessary that the husband and wife work out their relationship, have quality time together and are the primary care givers of their children.

Authority and Mutual Blessing Between Parents and Children

One of the greatest sources of human fulfillment in mutual blessing is between parents and children. There is an established authority and submission relationship between parents and their minor children. Children are told to honor their parents in the ten commandments and to obey their parents in Ephesians 6. However, parents are also told to not provoke their children to wrath but to bring them up in the fear and instruction of the Lord. Children are blessed by the overwhelming love that is intended for them. The level to which righteous and loving parents sacrifice for their children is enormous! It includes all the dimensions of working hard for material provision, making times for instruction, sharing principles in story telling, worshipping, joining in fun activities, and hugging and kissing with professions of love. The parents bless their children with love, wisdom, discipline, instruction, training and more. However, the children respond to the parents with love and obedience which, greatly blesses the parents. In addition, the adult children return appreciation and bless their parents with friendship, discussions to gain wisdom, grandchildren, and provision and care when the parents are old. Of course, we are speaking of an ideal here.

Once children come to understand right and wrong and have a clear conscience, they must not obey their parents when they know it to be contrary to the Word of God. This is true in all relationships of authority and submission. Children learn the true nature of authority from a godly Messiah like father. They learn the true nature of submission through a godly sanctified mother who is like the bride of the Messiah. We will be in roles of authority and submission through most of our lives, exercising authority and being under authority. It is through mothers and fathers and their relationship that children learn.

When parents watch their children grow and learn, there is particular delight. Thousands of looks and expressions as the children grow never cease to amaze and warm the heart. The children themselves enjoy the delight of discovering freedom provided by parents. At every age there are new mutual blessings. Indeed, children keep parents younger, for parents relive a youthful joy in doing things with their children that they otherwise might not do. As we watch our children learn at every age—as they swim, ride a bike, hit a baseball, and roller skate—their joy is truly our joy. Somehow, we recapture our youth through our children, but in a new way of fellowship with our children as they learn together, have sport together, and discover together.

However, this is the ideal. We are aware that parents struggle to be consistent in nurturing their children with love and faith. Parents and children face anger, unforgiveness, and withdrawal. Parents struggle when children are rebellious. Children struggle when parents are harsh and selfish. Both parents and children need to learn the way of the cross in mutual repentance and forgiveness to attain to the ideals of mutual blessing. There is pain in parenting, and the pain must be faced and worked through.

Minor children are to obey their parents, while children who reach adulthood relate to their parents with honor, receiving advice and counsel. Adult children are no longer in a relationship of obedience. It is very important for continued mutual blessing that parents and children change in their relationship as the children mature. In marriage the children should embrace leaving and cleaving. A new structure of family has been established which requires respect from the parents. The grandparents are not primary authorities over the grandchildren except as delegated by the parents. The wisdom of God and the love of God in creating families amazes and delights us.

The role of teachers and students is another example of mutual blessing. To younger children, teachers serve as surrogates for the parents. The parents are responsible for the education of their children, but delegate some of this to teachers who are especially capable in special subjects. The teachers are fulfilled in preparing the next generation for responsible and fulfilled living. They are enriched by the gratitude of their students. The students are enriched by the knowledge and wisdom received from teachers. Authority has something to give and submitted ones have something to receive. The submitted one, therefore, shows the respect of one receiving a gift. Even adults who submit to teachers should show an attitude of respect and submission reflecting an interdependence for mutual blessing. What a great profession teaching is! Of course, I am assuming godly teaching from people of godly character.

On Children and Family

My little one, whose tongue is dumb,
Whose fingers cannot hold to things,
Who is so mercilessly young,
He leavps upon the instant things
I hold him not, Indeed, who could?
He runs into the burning wood.

Follow, flow if you can!
He will come out grown to a man
And not remember whom he kissed,
Who caught him by the slender wrist
And bound him by a tender yoke
Which understanding not, he broke

Tennessee Williams

Civil Government and Authority

One of the blessings intended by God is the relationship to righteous civil government to a civilization. The purpose of civil government is given in Romans 13. Here, we read that the magistrate is present for the purpose of rewarding good behavior and punishing evil behavior. In this he does not wield the sword in vain if he is guided by this ideal. It is God who establishes the spheres of authority and submission and places people into leadership roles. Therefore, all are called to respect the magistrates and submit to their authority as long as it is not contrary to the Word of God. When direction is given that is contrary, then we "must obey God rather than man." We never are to violate the Word for any human authority. Of course, government can become demonic; it can treat its citizenry as only a means to enrich those in power. One can see the results in Russia where first the serfs were treated as slaves to enrich the nobility and then the population was used to enrich the leadership elite and to build the military-industrial complex of communism. However, most of the population continued to live at third-world levels. We see the kind of government that should be disobeyed illustrated by Nazi Germany. False theories of racial superiority were given credibility. Persecution of the Jewish people, and the few faithful Christians that supported them was beyond comprehension. Governmental authority that becomes demonic, as this example shows, is to be resisted. This is the image of Revelation 13. The prophets spoke against the great sin of unjust government. They called for justice in the courts of the land and righteousness in the leadership in general.

No human government in this age is perfect. However, there are times when rulers truly serve the people and seek to establish real justice. There are selfless public servants who put the good of the people above their own personal interest. Such a man was George Washington. He set a trajectory that blesses the United States to this day. How blessed are the people who have such governors and honest judges in the courts! Such men bless the people with order so that the future has some dependability. They can make plans, exercise creativity, worship in freedom, make contracts and produce wealth to benefit all. Without righteous government in a fallen world, violence and criminal elements destroy human security and advance. Righteous government officials gain great satisfaction in seeing a just and righteous social order established. They rejoice to see the people prosper. They are greatly blessed by the gratitude of the people. The people are blessed by all the benefits of righteous government; low crime, punishment of criminals, safety in the neighborhood, freedom of enterprise, freedom of religion, protection of free speech and material advance. Without good government, none of these blessings are possible. So true followers of the Word honor their governmental leaders. The police are treated with respect, for they are on the front line of wielding the sword for the people's good. Even if we are found in simple violations like a traffic *faux pas*, we should exercise gratitude. We should remember that traffic laws benefit all and provide the freedom for all of us to travel. Our respect is also shown in paying legitimate taxes, voting in a democracy and obeying regulations from housing codes to environmental protection laws. Where we believe that policy is not pragmatically the best, we can work in a respectful way to change policy, recognizing that we obey as long as the governmental law is not contrary to the Word of God.

No sphere of authority is independent of God. In the Bible, God claims authority over the whole universe and over every sphere of life. The wrong understanding of the separation of Church and State is dangerous. Such a state thinks that rights are given by the State and can be withdrawn by the State. Rather, rights are given by the Creator, as is stated in the US Declaration of Independence. Government is accountable to God in its sphere for its laws. The world-view of the people and the leadership of the state determine the understanding of the law of God and accountability to God. Without such accountability, government will become tyrannical. This accountability should be explicitly acknowledged by the state. The governmental sphere does not seek to establish religion, but to establish the conditions where it will flourish in freedom. Patriotism should be that commitment to a nation because of the greatness of the principles that are foundational in that nation.

The Employer and the Employee-Business Relationship

The Bible gives little information concerning employers and employees. In the New Testament we read of the relationship between masters and slaves. In the history of theology this is usually applied to the employer-employee relationship. The whole thrust of the Bible is toward freedom from bondage. Therefore, slavery was unknown among most believers by the end of the second century. In the Ephesians 6 passage that speaks about this, we are told that slaves are to serve their masters as if serving the Messiah. However, masters are to treat their slaves as fellow servants of the one Master Yeshua, even as brothers in the Messiah. We see this in Paul's letter to Philemon during his instruction to Philemon on how he is to treat his returning slave Onesimus. It eventually became impossible for believers to hold slaves when they were to receive them as equally created in the image of God and as brothers in the Lord. However, it does seem that the instructions have application for employees and employers.

In addition, the Torah does give instruction concerning paying employees a fair wage and not withholding wages for a day. It never defines a fair wage, but humane treatment for employees who are of benefit to the employer are part of the ethics of the Torah. This is also reflected in the prophets, who rail against oppression. We live in a vastly more complex order, having passed through the industrial age and now are in the beginnings of the information age. How shall we see these passages?

It still appears to many, this writer included, that the business sphere is an authority sphere where owner entrepreneurs and managers with employees enter into a contractual relationship. The owner and his managers exercise authority over employees. Basically, an owner of a business has accumulated sufficient wealth to start a business which produces a product or service that is to the benefit of others. In a biblical ethical context, only products and services that are to the real benefit of others are legitimate. There are businesses that make much money but believers should have nothing to do with them. These included, for example, pornography, violent entertainment, gambling concerns and foreign investments that return increase by slave labor. The business person has an idea that will take the risk of his capital to make this idea work. He hires employees who enter into a contract to submit to the leadership of the owner or managers to carry out the plans of the business owner. There is mutual blessing in the arrangement. Those with the gifts of entrepreneurial creativity provide jobs and provision for employees who may not have such gifts. However, the employer could not bring his ideas to fruition without the employees. Therefore, he seeks to gain an honest return on his risk, while blessing the employees with the financial increase from the sales of the product or service. Indeed, the enterprise also blesses the society with the service or product.

Ideally, relationship presumes that the employer will generously enrich the employee to the extent that he is able to live well while the employer gains a fair increase for his risk on investment and for his creative leadership that he provides for others. In addition, he seeks to balance competition, productivity and other factors in seeking to do this. The employee is not necessarily in a permanent given relationship of submission under an employer, for he is free to leave the company, enter into contract with another company or to start his own business if he has the capital and gifting. Michael Novak has a marvelous book in this regard entitled *Business as a Calling.*[1]

However, if working conditions are good and wages are fair, it is good to enable long-term service in one business.

---

1. Michael Novak, *Business as a Calling,* Free Press, New York, 1996.

Relationships and friendships may grow in this setting. New trends and competition in new information technologies seem to produce little stability or company loyalty. This can be a problem in long-term motivation.

As long as the employee is with the company, he is submitted to obey the directions of the employer and the managers over him, unless the directions contradict the Word of God. If the civil government, as the arbitrator of fair business practices, does not protect employees through laws and enforcement that support the employee in his legitimate expectation of fairness, and in his conscience for honest work that is in accord to his religious convictions, then it will be necessary to appeal to the employer. If the employer will not accommodate the conscience of the employee, then he may need to trust God for a new job where his convictions will not be compromised. This means that employers should not seek to make employees compromise adequate family time, time for duties to God and the religious sphere and time for recreation. There are laws being passed for such concerns. For example, Maryland state law requires employers to accommodate their employees with regard to a Sabbath day, either Friday (Muslim), Saturday (Jews and Adventists) or Sunday (Christians). In addition, labor unions seek to see larger corporations establish fair and just standards in these matters for just compensation.

Varieties of gifts are used in business corporations. All are important to the success of the enterprise. In the employer-employee relationship, we again see the principle of mutual blessing. Both are interdependent for mutual prosperity and the fulfillment of producing products and services that are of worth. In so doing, there is a sense of self-fulfillment and satisfaction. We are acting creatively together. New methods of production where the employee sees the fruit of his labor rather than just impersonally turning a wrench are well in keeping with the biblical emphasis on the dignity of man. Indeed, new modes of car manufacturing are a case in point. Ideally, we are to enjoy our work, though the fall brought thorns and impediments to success. We are not to expect to always have an ideal situation in this life.

Authority and Blessing in the Congregational Sphere

We have an overwhelming problem in congregations today. It is that people have lost reverence for authority in general and especially in this sphere. The congregational sphere is to be the source of blessing and discipleship for people that they might understand all the other spheres of mutual blessing and authority. In this sphere, people find God's order and fulfillment and become responsible disciples. However, if authority in the congregational sphere is not understood, it will have the most awesome negative implication for all of life. Why? Because it is the foundational sphere of authority against whatYeshua taught: that the gates of hell would not prevail (Matthew 16).

One of the great problems since the Reformation is the fragmentation of this sphere. The Reformers had little choice but to bring their message and call for change to the Church of their day. However, they envisioned one reformed church that would call the Catholic and Orthodox Churches back to biblical standards. Even then, when one particular church was predominant in various countries (Reformed in Holland and Scotland, Lutheran in Germany and Scandinavia, Anglican in England) there was still a more unified sphere of ecclesiastical government in every locale. However, the late 19th century brought forth a plethora of unnecessary fragmentation, and the 20th century accelerated this fragmentation, not because of doctrinal difference, but because of style and the concept of the independent local church. This is an idea that is foreign to the Bible, for in the Bible there is only one congregation in every locale, even if it meets in different gatherings. There is only one city eldership for each city. In addition, Yeshua prayed that we might be one that the world might believe (John 17:21). This unity must be expressed in some type of cooperative effort and mutuality in government over the city together. The fear of unity, as if our unity is only to be ethereal and mystical, is simply wrong. Heart unity must lead to visible and practical unity. Thank God that there are such efforts today to overcome the fragmentation of believers.

The basic authority in the life of the Body of Believers is the eldership. These elders might serve as overseers of the city with a leading elder as moderator. Also, local assemblies might have local assembly elders. According to the Scriptures, members are to submit to the elders (I Peter 5), and in one passage (Hebrews 13:17) are called to obey them. We also see evidence that in every eldership there is a first among equals to give leadership to the elders and help them to come to unity in vision and implementation. This is because the gift of leadership itself comes in greater and lesser capability. Elders may express different combinations of gifts according to Ephesians 4:11ff. These are apostles, prophets, evangelists, pastors and teachers, who are to equip the saints for the work of ministry (service) until we come to the unity of the faith and grow up into mature men unto the stature of the fullness of the Messiah. Understanding these types of gifting can help us not put people into wrong roles, being miscast, and frustrating themselves and the people. Immediately, we can see the features of mutual blessing. The elders are to equip the people so they might fulfill their destinies in God.

In addition, elders bring discipline to the unruly and those who bring false doctrine or immoral life patterns into the congregation of God. They are instructed to maintain a basic unity and purity in the life of the Body and to see that those who practice gross sin are to be removed (I Cor. 5:11ff.). Matthew 18:15ff, as described before, gives the basic pattern of congregational discipline.

When a congregation has godly elders and is willing to follow their leadership, great blessing follows for all. First of all, there is mutual blessing between God and the congregation. He is the one who fills us with his Spirit and blesses us with anointing to be effective for his Kingdom. He rejoices in a righteous and effective people, and he rejoices the hearts of his people with the presence of his love. As the corporate bride of the Messiah, we are in a love feast of delight in him. However, this bride is ordered under elders and apostolic leaders who tie congregations and cities together in a larger unity. (We believe in a restoration model of government where senior five-fold leaders form councils to oversee congregations.)

Let us look at some of the passages that describe submission and authority between the elders and the people.

To the elders among you, I appeal as a fellow elder, a witness of Messiah's suffering and one who will share in the glory to be revealed. Be shepherds of God' flock that is under your care, serving as overseers--not because you must, but because you are willing, as God wants you to be, not greedy for money, but eater to serve, not lording it over those entrusted to you, but being examples to the flock. And when the Chief Shepherd appers, you will receive the crown of glory that will never fade away.

Young men, in the same way, be submissive to those whoa re older. All of you clothe yourselves with humility toward one another because, "God opposes the proud, but gives greace to the humble." (I Peter 5:1-5, NIV)

Obey your leaders and submit to their authority. They keep watch over you as men who must give an account. Obey them so that their work will be a joy, not a burden, for that woudl be of no advantage to you. (Hebrews 13:17, NIV)

In addition, we can see from I Timothy 3 that elders are to be men who have proven themselves in leading their marriages and families. Governing in righteousness with love is the key qualification. It is well to read the passage as a whole to see the nature of God's requirements.

Here is a trustworthy saying, If anyone sets his heart on being an overseer, he desires a noble task. Now the overseer must be above reproach, the husband of but one wife, temperate, self-controlled, respectable, hospitable, able to teach, not givven to drunkenness, not violent but gentle, not quarrelsome, not a lover of money. He must manage his own family well and see that his children obey him with proper respect. (If anyone does not know how to manage his own famiy, how can he take care of God's church?) He must not be a recent convert or he may become conceited and fall under the same judgment as the devil. He must also have a good reputation with outsiders, so that he will not fall into disgrace and into the devil' trap. (I Tim. 3:1-7, NIV)

The requirements for deacons are also high and similar to elders (I Tim. 3:8-12). Whether the deacons teach, lead small groups, distribute aid, or oversee programs, they serve the elders and by doing so aid them in establishing the government of God.

The weight of these passages show how far we are from the biblical idea. Generally, we understand that the members have freedom of conscience before the Word of God. Elders must not impose upon their members so as to destroy their families and the time required for this sphere, or to impose upon a normal involvement in the business sphere. However, we have come to a place where there is little submission or obedience to elders for the most part. Yes, when elders ask for too much there should be an appeal. What if the elders ask all to be present for an important meeting unless they have crucial reasons to not do so? In most congregations, there is such a lazy individualism that only a minority will submit to the call of the elders. What if the elders ask all to take course for membership? Many will attend a congregation but never obey the standards for membership. People shop for a congregation like shopping for a car rather than finding the place of the call of God to serve. That place may be the one where there is need for help and not where everything functions with the order of a McDonald's fast food restaurant. Rather, people should find a community where they can serve in submission to an eldership.

It would seem that if a congregation sets a reasonable standard for involvement, that most of the members will follow it if they read the Scriptures on submission and obedience. Let's say weekly attendance, cell group attendance and an area of service are part of membership; this should bring almost total compliance. We cannot move together in power and accomplishment with so much individualism. What if all are called to serve the lost in some way as part of congregational life? Isn't this why we are here? I am not asking for congregational discipline to be enjoined upon members in such a way that we become authoritarian. Teaching the Word of God should contribute to the ideal that congregations would move together as one body. In the life of a congregation there should be minimal standards for members in good standing and greater requirements for leaders. Today, congregations are simply treated as service providers where people attend until they sense a need for different or better services. This is not biblical, but people are called to become part of a community expressed in small group cells where they share life and accountability together. Movement out should only be by the real leading of the Spirit. (We believe that small groups or cells are biblically mandated. They are overseen by the elders. Only then can there be participatory meetings as described in I Cor. 12 and 14.)

When a congregation is functioning rightly, there is tremendous blessing or mutual enrichment between the elders and the members, the deacons and the elders, and the deacons and the members. The elders receive joy in the gratitude from the members for their having discipled them and equipped them to find the Kingdom of God. The elders and deacons receive joy in seeing the Kingdom of God extended by creating a community of faith that is effective. When they see people healed and restored, marriages and families become healthy and lost people are won to the Kingdom. In this there is great joy. This is why the writer of Hebrews exhorts the congregations to make the job of the Shepherds one with joy and not with grief (Hebrews 13:17). The members and their shepherds are in a joyful bonded relationship. In addition, members receive the joy of seeing their submission produce growth and fruit in their lives. By submitting to be equipped and trained to follow the Word of God, members maximize their effectiveness in the Kingdom. As the congregation gathers for worship and teaching, the presence of the Spirit brings great corporate joy. Of course the Congregation, or the sphere of the Church, is the center of mutual blessing corporately between man and God! He provides all for the congregation, and we bless him in our worship, love, gratitude, and service.

Membership in a congregation is a covenant commitment. We should not leave or transfer unless we really know the leading of the Spirit to do so. Ideally, we are sent with confirmation. It is painful to be called out if our relationships are deep. This is the ideal. To show humility in our hearing the Spirit, we seek confirmation as a guard against subjective mistakes, but are freed to be affirmed even if we do not get confirmation for directions in our personal lives. The leading of the Spirit and wise counsel are the biblical answers to destructive mobility in the body. Too many members change congregations too often: too many move away and never build long term relationships; too many abandon friends and families. It is important to teach on the ideal of stable relationships, and on the hearing of the Spirit. If we disciple a mature person and train them to hear from God, that person will only move when it is genuinely the leading of the Spirit. The Spirit will not lead to destructive mobility. In my view a minority of decisions of moving are really from God; though people say, "The Spirit told me," they do whatever they want to do. Only discipleship and accurate hearing of the Spirit can be bulwark against these destructive trends.

So in congregational life, we see the wonderful mutual enrichment between God and the Congregation and between elders and people. Authority has something to give to the people. The people have something to receive. Authority pours out sacrificially that the people might benefit. Then the people have something to give in return. All authority among believers in every sphere is never for power's sake or to Lord it over others. It is rather a type of heavier responsibility and greater sacrifice for the good of all. The authority of leaders does not only depend on recognizing an office, for this will only last so long, but upon developing the loving relationship that is also needed. This is why Yeshua speaks of servant leadership.

Timothy Dwight, President of Yale in the early 19th century wrote the hymn I love thy Kingdom Lord, on his love for the Church. The reader should read the word house to be the gathered people, not the building.

> I love Thy kingdom, Lord,
> The house of Thine abode,
> The church our blessed Redeemer saved
> With His own precious blood.
> I love Thy church, O God.
> Her walls before Thee stand,
> Dear as the apple of Thine eye,
> And written on Thy hand.
> If e'er to bless Thy sons
> My voice or hands deny,
> These hands let useful skills forsake,
> This voice in silence die.
> Should I with scoffers join
> Her altars to abuse?
> No! Better far my tongue were dumb,
> My hand its skill should lose.
> For her my tears shall fall
> For her my prayers ascend,
> To her my cares and toils be given
> Till toils and cares shall end.
> Beyond my highest joy
> I prize her heavenly ways,
> Her sweet communion, solemn vows,
> Her hymns of love and praise.
> Jesus, Thou friend divine,
> Our Savior and our king,

Thy hand from every snare and foe
Shall great deliverance bring.
Sure as Thy truth shall last,
To Zion shall be given
The brightest glories earth can yield
And brighter bliss of Heaven.

The Spheres of Authority in
Mutual Blessing to One Another

The spheres of authority and submission in human society are not sealed off from one another. For example, the separation of church and state as presently interpreted by the courts of the United States presents an impossible, artificial and dangerous interpretation. This is because the state is accountable to God in its sphere. No sphere is free from God. It is just that the state is not responsible to establish a particular denomination. However, the morality that informs the laws of the state is based on religious or world-view convictions. The founders of the United States understood that the strength of the country was in its religious-moral foundations. So argued George Washington, John Adams and many others. So also today argues conservative Rabbi Dennis Praeger. In addition, not all religious practices are acceptable. The state may proscribe religious freedom when it is grossly against the moral consensus and the law of the land. For example, the state should not allow the practice of the caste systems of India or slavery in our land even if these are religious convictions. Child sacrifice is definitely against the law though practiced by some religions. The State blesses the religious sphere with a society of justice and freedom within limits so that it might be free to operate congregations and to seek to persuade others to their convictions. The religious sphere provides the state with trustworthy citizens and people of character to serve in civil government. So the two spheres are mutually interdependent and bless one another. This is the implication of Paul's exhortation in I Timothy 2 that we pray for civil leaders that we might have a just government and live a peaceable life.

We can also see that the business sphere blesses the religious sphere, for it provides the income that people give to support the religious sphere. The religious sphere trains its members for responsible involvement in the business realm. Owners and employees follow the patterns of integrity taught by the congregation from the Word of God.

In addition, the civil sphere blesses the business sphere so that there might be fair rules of competition and a winning situation for worthy businesses and those that benefit by their services and products. The laws of contracts, antimonopoly laws, rational environmental regulations, union rights and much more make the business sphere humane and ultimately bless all. The business sphere creates the wealth to support the civil sphere, the police, the courts and more.

It is obvious that the family also is interdependent with all the others and receives blessing and gives blessing. A sound and just civil sphere makes the raising of good families easier. Good families are the key to multiplying more good families in the sphere of the congregation. Both provide the character training for people to serve in other spheres.

It is awesome to contemplate the inter-relatedness and distinction of spheres of authority and the ideal of mutual blessing that is to flow from this.

Chapter VI:

Gifts and Talents in Blessing

God distributes gifts and talents in his sovereignty. Though we enjoy being used in our gifts and talents, these gifts and talents are for the benefit of others, given to us by God to create an interdependence of mutual blessing. The passage in Ephesians 4:11 speaks of the gifts given through five-fold leaders. There are apostles, prophets, evangelists, pastors and teachers. Each is said to equip the saints for the work of ministry. Leadership gifts enable others to fulfill their destinies. Apostles establish new congregations, oversee congregations and lay foundations of doctrine and practice. Prophets see direction from God and submit their hearing to the elders to enable a supernatural dimension to God's leading. They equip the saints to hear from God and to be a prophetic people. In addition, evangelists equip the saints to effective witness. It is not only a matter of their public preaching but blessing the whole congregation with equipping. In addition, pastors see that the flock is cared for and that they grow in spiritual stability and fulfillment. Equipping by the pastor brings the congregation to being a caring shepherding congregation. The teacher effects the congregation so that it is well taught. When this is done, congregational members can teach new members. Leaders are blessed by the success of the people of God. The congregation is blessed to come into effectiveness in many dimensions. The people find blessing not only in relational friendship with leaders but in the joy of fulfilling their destiny and in the fulfillment of their potential.

We can see deeper meaning through the Scriptures when we read, "Whoever receives a prophet as a prophet receives a prophet's reward." (Matt. 10:41). The prophet brings a blessing to the one who receives him, a reward that is equal to the reward of the prophet who brings the gift.

However, it is not only leadership gifts, but many other gifts by which there is mutual blessing. The Scriptures list several gifts of utterance and then other manifestations of the Spirit. They include tongues, interpretation of tongues, prophecy, the discernment of spirits, wisdom, knowledge, faith, gifts of healing and the effecting of miracles (I Cor. 12:8ff.). The verse preceding the list says that to each is given the manifestation of the Spirit for the common good. Here is an ideal rarely practiced. Because the gathered community is interdependent, all are to contribute a manifestation of the Spirit to build up the whole community and every individual member of it. Theoretically, because all have the Spirit, all could move in any of these gifts and manifestations. However, though many express more than one gift, God has so apportioned the gifts that we are again interdependent! He purposely distributes in such a way that we will need one another to see the gathering of the Spirit take place. Again, mutual blessing is in mind. Those with seemingly greater gifts cannot succeed without those with supposedly lesser gifts. If all the members of the community come into their gifts and practice them for the common good, the mutual enrichment will be amazing. This is God's plan and way that each individual can find blessing in seeing the Spirit move through them, and all members may receive the blessing of those gifts. Those with greater gifting are only possessing these gifts to bless others. It is not for pride or selfish ambition. All can rejoice in what they receive. The mutual gift mix in our gatherings is part of the Temple reality of the body of the Messiah, the Temple in which the Spirit dwells.

Romans 12 gives another list of what some have called motivational gifts. This is not a book on the gifts of the Spirit. There are many wonderful books on this. It is on the *Theology of Mutual Blessing.*. Apostles and prophets have already been discussed. The purpose of teaching has been made clear. The list also includes serving, exhortation, giving, showing mercy and administration (or leading). The context here is not the same as the gathered community context of I Corinthians 12. The exhorter, for example, will encourage others toward victory. He is a motivator that others might fulfill their destiny. This may be done both on an individual and a corporate level. Ones who do works of mercy also may serve in many contexts of need. The administrator or leader will organize people together in such a way that the maximum use of the calling of each can be used to the benefit of all and to the effective extension of the Kingdom. The prophet may encourage the mercy person when he needs direction or confidence in a situation of challenge. However, the mercy person may greatly aid the prophet when he or she is tired, sick or in need of encouragement from the great rejection that prophets often receive. Each gifted person may bless all the other persons in different giftings. All are again blessed in an amazing mutual accountability and mutual enrichment.

The Word in I Corinthians 12 is again most pertinent. Because the eye and the hand are not the same, neither can one say to the other member, "I have no need of you." The whole congregational body needs all of its members. In addition, the more unseemly parts of the body are needed and are to be the objects of special care just as in the case of the physical body. Love is to tie all together in this mutual blessing. All are commanded to desire the best gifts for the building up of the body. However, we are to seek the way of love that our gifts may not be sources of pride but genuine expressions of love for the sake of enriching the other.

ARTISTS AND MUTUAL BLESSING

Many have pointed out, especially Dorothy Sayers in *The Mind of the Maker,* that creativity is one of the most important human attributes whereby we see that human beings are created in the image of God.[1] God is creative and so are human beings!

It is not only the gifts of the Spirit in the supernatural sense that bring blessing, but the many different talents that are apportioned to God's people. Let us for example take the person who is greatly talented in visual art. While I appreciate art, I am far from being a great artist. However, great art awakens us to the wonder, mystery, and grandeur of life. It may also awaken us to the tragic nature of existence or to a deep

---

1. Dorothy Sayers, **The Mind of the Maker,** first published 1941, Harper edition, New York, 1978.

perception of the human condition. For example, the paintings of Turner from England strike me as especially wonderful in showing the grandeur and power of nature. Paintings are not just photographic reproductions, but interpretations that help us to see beyond our usual perception. Poems are the same. Wordsworth helps us to see the wonder of creation in a way that no scientific material description can. His meditations in poetry open us to see beyond our usual bland orientation. His meditations at Tinturn Abby, or Tennyson's poems on the nature of faith, or T. S. Elliot on faith and modern life, open up profound insight.

The poet is blessed by being appreciated for his work and by being an instrument of deeper perception, almost revelation. The patron of the poet is blessed to receive the understanding that he would have not received on his own. He is blessed to have financed something beautiful or true through the artist. The artist is blessed by his patron so he can fulfill his destiny as an artist.

Poems by Edith Juster, my mother, 1916-2002

God Surrounded Him
(This poem is a true story as noted by Edith)

I walked along one day in a town called Hackensack
I waited for a bus; the bench one sits on was full of ice
Along came a black man, his face so sweet so tender
He was not young, but I sensed that God surrounded him
He brushed the ice with his bare hands and said
Please sit and rest

I felt so strange, his face so good
As though God surrounded him

He stood in line when the bus came, a long line
The he stepped out and gave me his place
Even though I said, you must not
He walked to the back of the line

When I left the bus, he too did leave
"Thank you", I whispered in awe
I felt I saw sorrow, beauty and kindness
As though surrounded by God's presence

I watched him go, what man is this
He walked into a church and I felt that God had touched me
Why? To show me some deep love through him, this lonely
black man
He left an aura of sweetness; I think God is telling me
something
Lord show me what it is
Such tenderness is you

Written in December of 1972

To My Mother 1937

God must have visioned his greatest make
Flowers and trees did surely quake

With the thought of such loneliness
Lonelier than they, this women he now was about to array
With a soul so beautiful and a face so sweet
Angels flocked to be there to meet

And played on their harps such a melodious time

The dew kissed rose in the month of June
Reverently lifted her head to say
Oh God! Let all the world pray today

For she had eyes that could fill with the deepest tears
Smiles that could wipe away all our fears
Hands so tender to ease great pain
For those who suffering long had lain

This was the Mother he gave to the earth
And yet how little I've proved my worth

Again, we are all artists to some small degree, but great artists enter into a role of mutual blessing with all who can receive their art, the consumers of art. Truth, beauty and goodness are revealed in more profound ways through the artist. How blessed is he to receive such understanding and blessed to be appreciated! However, the greatest blessing is received by those who benefit by appreciating the work of art and rejoice. Today, art has fallen on hard times. Many do not believe that there is any objective truth, beauty, or goodness to be revealed. However, great art that will survive the generations sufficiently demonstrates one or more of these dimensions of ultimate meaning. Art that does not have such greatness will simply be forgotten. The realm of art is therefore a most important calling for a significant number of followers of Yeshua.

The Realm of Sports

The Realm of Sports is a subset of aesthetics. It also partakes of the aspect of drama, which is a reflection of truth and beauty. The athlete who performs well shows the glory of God in the coordination of physical beauty and mental discipline. We see this in the runner, skier, and especially the gymnast. The ice skater projects an amazing and special beauty. These represent the excellence of the individual competitor. In addition, excellent execution in team sports such as basketball, baseball, soccer and football can fill us with wonder. The coordinated beauty is to the glory of God as creator. Michael Novak, in *The Joy of Sports,* connects the meaning of sports to everlasting life and play.[2] We enjoy sports because of the drama involved. Which team will win? The home team is portrayed as the good team and the away team as the bad team. When the home team is losing and has a come from behind victory in the last minutes of the quarter or in the last inning of the game in a dramatic ending, we are thrilled. It is the kind of thing fans live to see. Does this connect to something deep in our consciousness concerning the nature of reality and the ultimate victory of the righteous people of God (the home team) when it seems most hopeless? Does not God pull us out in the last minute many times? When the ending is dramatic, it is most amazing. Cal Ripkin, the famous baseball player, was a player with very good character, played with excellence toward the end of his career and beat Lou Gehrig's consecutive games played record (considered a record that would never be broken). Ted Williams hit a home run in his last at bat in his last game. Babe Ruth hit two home runs in his last game. Willie Mays returned to New York, where he had the greatest following, though his former team abandoned New York for San Francisco. He contributes in his

---

2. Michael Novak, **The Joy of Sports,** Madison Books, Toronto, Canada, 1976, 1994

last year to a National League Pennant for the New York Mets. What was it like when our High School won the state football championship in the last minute on a chilly November Day in 1963? What was it like when Gaithersburg High School in Maryland won the 1998 state basketball championship after five overtimes? It was thrilling beyond description! One of our congregational members was the captain of the team and the contingent from our congregation proved to be the most intense fan club. There is a special quality in amateur sports since those involved play for the love of the game and not for money.

The athlete is blessed by the excellence of his execution. He is blessed by the gratitude of the fans. The fans are blessed by their identification with the athlete, the team etc. They rejoice in the beauty and the drama and are sometimes deepened by empathy with the tragic dimension of sports. One who follows a team for years and experiences their defeat, is especially blessed when the team wins. This was much more the case when sports teams were stable in composition, before free agency and big dollars. Athletes are blessed with talents that bless the athlete and others.

We can see that the whole nature of gifts and talents shows forth God's principles. God in his sovereignty distributes gifts and talents. Gifts and talents can be developed by the person who receives them. Gifts and talents are to be exercised for the blessing of others. In such a way, we again become interdependent for mutual blessing. One with fewer talents has less responsibility but still serves with what he or she has and can receive the fullness of what has been given to others. Less talented people live to the praise and glory of

God by creating a beautiful life in the context of lesser talents. Proportions of gifts and talents are never for the purpose of comparing one another or for egocentric orientations. Rather they are for servanthood. We are all in an order of giving and receiving.

Chapter VII:

Blessing Through Words

The Bible puts forth a view of words that goes well beyond the conception of the contemporary secularists. Indeed, to some secularists a word is only a sign that signifies a material object, and only material objects exist. However, in Scripture words can both hide reality (if they are the wrong words) and can disclose reality (if they are the right words). Love, guilt, conscience, the mind, self-reflection, the sense of wonder and mystery, the perception of Divinity, and more are experienced in part by what words convey. Yet every human experience is more than words can express. Nevertheless, words are the vehicles whereby we communicate our common experiences to one another.

More than this, the world according to the Bible is filled with powers: angels, demons, princes of darkness, and God himself. In God's arrangement of reality, words are power packets. Some words may have little power, but no word has no power. Words may "fall to the ground" or have little effectiveness. Or words may be powerful and bring about what is proclaimed. Meredith Kline, the noted Old Testament professor from

Gordon-Conwell Divinity School, has extensively studied the prophets of the Bible and concluded that the words decreed were part of bringing about what was proclaimed. It is not just that the prophet announces what God is going to do, and that God would do it with or without the announcement. It is that the announcement of the prophet is part of releasing the power to bring it about. The prophet's word is God's word which will not return void. Words, therefore, are seen as having substance! This is especially the case with God's own creation words. "By the Word of the Lord the heavens were made and all the host by the breath of his mouth. ... He spoke and it was done, He commanded, and it stood fast" (Psalm 33:6,9, NKJ). Even so Yeshua healed by the command of his word.

We can find many other examples of the God-inspired power of words. Moses speaks to the rock to bring forth water (or at least he was supposed to do this). Elijah pronounces drought and announces rain. Moses pronounces the plagues before they come upon Egypt. The prophets in the book of Revelation 11 bring about plagues as often as they desire by the command of their mouths.

The most important release of power in words in the Bible is the power of blessing. We are called to bless others and not to curse. Paul noted that this was his practice, to bless even those who curse us. If the righteous are cursed, it may come back on the one who speaks it. If the righteous bless, the blessing becomes ours as well and even rebounds to us from one who is undeserving.

Aaron was commanded to bless the children of Israel with these words, "The LORD bless you and keep you. The LORD make his face shine upon you and be gracious unto you. The

LORD lift up his countenance upon you and give you peace" (Numbers 6:24-24, NKV). Was this just a prayer that God may or may not answer? Or in normal circumstances, did not the priest release the very power of what they proclaimed? The priests lift up their hands so as to release upon the people what they say. Indeed, God is committing himself to do what is proclaimed in the blessing. The words of men bring the real blessing of God; we are partners of God in blessing. That the LORD makes his face to shine upon us and lifts up his countenance upon us is poetic parallelism. Both are different ways of releasing the greatest gift of all upon the Israelites. This is the very presence of God in a wonderful and perceived way.

Many other blessings can be spoken. May the LORD bless you, we might say, with long life, healing, prosperity, discernment, wisdom, and more. The prayer of Paul for the Ephesians is a type of blessing, "That the God of our Lord Jesus Christ, the Father of glory, may give to you the spirit of wisdom and revelation in the knowledge of him ... that you may know ... what is the exceeding greatness of His power toward us who believe (Ephesians 1:17-19, NIV). We see many such blessings all through the Scriptures. How great is his heritage in us and our heritage in him? These blessings essentially takes us into a new realm of living in the awareness of his supernatural presence and power; a sense of heaven in our present existence.

The patriarchs speak their dying blessings upon their children. These blessings are prophetic and creative. Jacob especially speaks to his eleven sons and makes his grandsons Ephraim and Manassah equal to them. These blessings come to fruition in the life of the tribes in ancient Israel.

The nature of blessing is God's way for us to speak good into the world. God expects us to be the source of blessing to others by our words and deeds. Not only so, but we are to bless God in all things and in doing so we enrich the life of God, and he enriches our lives. Indeed, when we bless God in a lavish way, we grow to perceive the mystery, wonder and grandeur of life. We see the mystery of God behind all things. In traditional Judaism, we are taught to say a blessing over the bread and the wine. "Blessed are you LORD our God, King of the Universe, who brings forth the bread from the earth," and "Blessed are you LORD God, King of the Universe, who creates the fruit of the vine." We are also taught to say a blessing over seeing anything wonderful. This includes a flower, an ocean, a rainbow or any miracle. Blessings are said over a bride and groom in a wedding. "Blessed are you LORD our God, who has created bride and bridegroom. Blessed are you who has created joy and gladness, love and brotherhood and peace." (From the Jewish wedding ceremony)

In the Jewish tradition we say *Kaddish* so that we bless God and affirm his goodness even in the face of death. "Glorified and sanctified be God's great name in the world which He has created according to His word. May He establish His Kingdom during your days and during the whole house of Israel, and say you, Amen."

Words of blessing and praise both to God and man provide the soil for faith. When blessing and gratitude characterize our relationships with others, there is an atmosphere of acceptance in which we can grow. The husband who constantly praises and blesses his wife establishes the climate in which his wife can grow into all God intends for her. The wife that blesses her husband gives him a sense of being appreciated and motivates him to love even more.

One of the most noted prayers in Judaism comes from the first century. It is known as the *Amidah*. Originally this prayer contained 18 blessings. Each one blesses God for either an aspect of his character or for what he has promised to do. It is a faith confession that blesses God as having for what has been promised as a certain reality. This includes healing the sick, raising the dead, rebuilding Jerusalem and establishing the Kingdom in the Age to Come. It includes restoring Israel as well. For all of these promises, God is blessed as though it is already done for he will certainly do it.

We have in recent years come to see that the messages we give one another and to our children especially are received as either a blessing or a curse. Derek Prince has written a fine book on this entitled *Blessing or Curse*.[1] Generalized statements spoken by parents to their children of a negative critical nature can scar the personality of the children. Statements by teachers, school mates, friends, and siblings have a significant effect as well. Sometimes a person curses himself. These curses need to be broken in the name of Yeshua and replaced by receiving the words of blessing that come through the Word of God.

The Scriptures enjoin us to "Bless those who curse us," and to "love our enemies." Paul professed to live out this command. When we bless another who is doing wrong, it does not mean that we want them to prosper in such a way that they will continue to be blind in complacency. Rather, we are praying for them to know the fellowship, joy and presence of

---

1. Derek Prince, **Blessing or Curse**, Chosen Books, Grand Rapids, Michigan, 1990.

God. This is the greatest blessing of all. However, this cannot be received if there is no repentance for serious sin, because serious sin produces a barrier between the person and God. Our blessing sometimes is in the form of, "May they repent that they might be blessed." Blessing our enemies never means praying for them to succeed or prosper in doing evil.

In all of this, we can see that our words have real power. We are to speak nothing contrary to the promises of God. In this we have the blessing of God.

Is there ever a time that we are to bring a curse to another? Yes, it biblically seems so. This can only be in cases where one who is captured by evil is doing horrible things against others. Then under the guidance of the Holy Spirit and for the sake of others, never for self, a curse can be spoken. This is reflected in the Psalms and in some of the words of the prophets which were inspired by God. However, this is an exceptional case.

Chapter VIII:

Blessing And Sacrament

O n of the interesting debates in the historic Church concerned the number of sacraments. Sacraments are ritual physical actions with words ordained by God for the reception of special effective grace. The churches of the Reformation said there were two, Baptism and Communion (the Eucharist and the Lord's Supper are other terms). Some post Reformation churches did not want to see any physical act as a means of receiving the grace of God, so they called Baptism and the Lord's Supper ordinances because they were seen as only reminders or symbolic testimonies. I am in agreement with the sacramentalists. It seems contrary to Scriptural emphasis to say that these acts are only witnesses when the testimony of Mark 16:15 says that "He that believes and is baptized shall be saved." In addition, those who take the Messiah's elements of bread and wine in an unworthy way are in danger of death or sickness according to I Corinthians 11. Something more is going on here than just a symbolic memorial. Rather this is an act that renews God's grace and power in our lives and the very meaning of his sacrificial death and resurrection. Ancient peoples including the Jewish people believe they receive the reality of what is portrayed in symbolic action.

Therefore, we can see that engaging in the Messiah's Supper and in the immersion in water we receive great blessing from God. Physical elements are used in a context whereby real spiritual blessing is conferred. This is in accord with both Lutheran and Reformed thought. However, the Lutherans believed that the elements of Communion become spiritually the body and blood of Yeshua. This doctrine is called the real presence. In Reformed thought, the act of participation is a means of God's conveying the grace of what is portrayed in the symbol. In Catholic and Orthodox Christian thought, the bread becomes the literal body of the Lord, and the wine becomes his literal blood. It is not my purpose to argue for my point of view on this. Suffice it to say that in the symbol of water immersion and in the symbol of bread and wine, we do really see the physical used to convey real enrichment to the participants, both corporately and individually. They receive the reality of what is portrayed by faith.

What of the other sacraments claimed by the Catholics and Orthodox believers? Let's look at them. First is marriage. Do we receive the life of God in marriage? The description of marriage as a reflection of the relationship between Yeshua and his Congregation brings us to see sacramental possibilities. If marriage is a covenant between a man and a woman before God and is a symbol of Yeshua and his people as described in Ephesians 5, it would seem quite acceptable to see it as sacramental. Is not special grace received in marital love when such love is expressed in a holy way in consciousness that it is a participation in the meaning of the Messiah and his Congregation? This is a wonderful blessing as described earlier.

What of the laying on of hands? This is usually claimed to be the sacrament of ordination. It would seem that the laying on of hands in ordination does convey the grace of God for fulfilling the call recognized in ordination. However, we lay hands on the sick as well, so healing virtue and grace are conveyed thereby.

Then, there is the sacrament of anointing with oil. This is for the healing of the physical body. According to James, the sick one is to call for the elders who will anoint him with oil. He is to confess his sins, and they will be forgiven. In faith, the sick one is expected to be healed. So it certainly would seem that the oil conveys a real grace and is a symbol of conveying Holy Spirit power that applies the virtue of Yeshua's cross to the sick. We read in Isaiah that we are healed by his stripes.

We can see here that the laying on of hands and anointing with oil both convey the power of the Holy Spirit. The Hebrew Scriptures describe anointing with oil for ordination. Some, therefore, use both oil and the laying on of hands for both healing and ordination.

Celibacy is also seen as a sacrament, a special vow where grace is received to serve the Lord in a special way in single life. However, it is harder to see a physical ritual here that conveys a special grace. This is also a hard one for Protestants and Messianic Jews.

William Temple in his great classic, *Nature, Man and God*, gave a wonderful presentation of sacrament as the nature of existence in this life. While we might see certain Scriptural acts as special sacraments, Temple argued that we live in a sacramental universe. We receive empowering grace through a right connection with the physical universe and perceiving the mystery and glory of God in it. In Judaism, the blessing over bread at a meal connects us to God and conveys grace. So enjoying the beauty of nature or even communion with a pet may also connect us to the wonder of our Creator and convey grace. Grace comes in raising and loving children or in myriads of other activities. The ordinary can be charged with the grace of God and be a means of conveying him to us. This is the blessing of life in God. What a wonderful way to see existence! Even tragedy can connect us to his comfort and be a source of grace as we realize eternal issues and perspectives. However, it is also important to note that the other rituals accepted as sacraments in the history of the Church are of a higher order and are designated as sacraments.

Chapter IX:

God's Order of Being, The Kingdom Of God

W here God rules, there is his Kingdom. God's Kingdom order is that which maximizes mutual enrichment or blessing for all people, all of nature, and God himself. The Jewish and biblical tradition calls this the order of Torah. The Gospel is the offer of the Kingdom of God that we can live in and form the Kingdom of God since the coming of Yeshua. When we embrace the Gospel, God works to put our lives in right order. This order is according to universal Torah. After Yeshua announced the Kingdom in Matthew 4, he made it clear in Matthew 5 that this Kingdom order is according to Torah (Matthew 5:17,18). "For out of Zion shall forth the Torah and the Word of the Lord from Jerusalem" (Isaiah 2).

Our fulfillment comes from finding our destiny in God's order of being that begins with "Loving God with all our heart, soul, strength, and mind" (Mark 12, Deuteronomy 6:4). Loving our neighbor as ourselves is the second great command in this order. The order of Torah begins in love which prefers the other. Love is the passionate identification with the other that seeks their good. Love is guided by the law of God, for people can only find their true fulfillment according to the declared will of God. Love perceives the worth of the other created in the image of God. The understanding of the image of God is a key to the Kingdom order of love. The cross is the center of this order, for it can only be attained when we die.

'The Scriptures teach that there are orders of being, some forms of life are higher and some forms lower in significance and meaning. It is amazing that the theory of naturalistic evolution has kept the Scriptural hierarchy of being in its scheme of natural development, making man the apex of the evolutionary process. Yet from a strictly evolutionary viewpoint there is no reason for human life to come about. High capabilities of survival and adaptation are already present among lower forms of life. Some lower forms of life are more adaptable then human beings. Science tells us that humans are more vulnerable than many species, so the survival of the fittest cannot possibly explain our existence. Though human life was first extolled in naturalism with man as the apex of evolution, we see that as time goes on, human life is being devalued. Without an understanding of God and creation and man's place in the order of being, there is a leveling effect to naturalism. This leveling takes place within the human society itself and in the orientation of man to nature. Let us first note the leveling taking place between man and nature.

It is crucial to understand man's responsibility for nature. He is to be a wise steward. If he ruins nature, he ruins his own life and the life of his descendants. It is amazing to note that Communism, which denied God, was the most environmentally destructive system in the 20th Century. Today, radical environmentalists deify nature. Professor Singer, now of Princeton, sees equal value to a dog and a fetus. Why? Because a dog has a more differentiated consciousness than a fetus according to Dr. Singer. Thus, we can kill a fetus without qualms. This supports the abortion movement, which denies the sacred value of the pre-born human person. In addition, environmentalists seek to preserve nature in a pristine state even if that is not necessary for nature's preservation and is negative for the improvement of human life. One animal rights activist stated that every animal species has as much right to life and happiness as the human species. There are some who believe that a world without human beings would be better. Human life really becomes cheapened.

In a society that does not believe in God or believe that man is created in his image and that on this basis that all men are equal, the crime rate grows dramatically. Fathers abandon families. Marriage is not even attempted. Children are raised without normal families and become more tempted to criminal behavior. The bonds of human trust break down. Lying, stealing and cheating become common. Science becomes compromised by political goals, and junk science is used to defend all sorts of socially destructive behaviors. (Junk science is speculation deceptively putting itself forth as if it were real science. Junk science violates the scientific criteria for evidence and proof. It draws conclusions with inadequate evidence.)

When we define living together without marriage as equal to marriage, raising children without fathers and mothers as equal to traditional families, and dogs as equal to fetuses, the results are a horrid leveling. Instead of all men created equal before God as Jefferson penned, we no longer can make distinctions. As Hitler thought, why not kill the handicapped since they do not live a good quality life or are not productive? There is no argument against Hitler's views without God. As Neitzche said, "If God is dead all things are possible." Why wouldn't it be valid to see one race as inferior and rightly eliminated by another? Civilized behavior is a much more fragile reality than we understand. Motivated by self-centered hedonistic orientations to life, contemporary society is destroying the fabric of a meaningful and stable human existence.

We see the same leveling in male and female roles. Women can be in military combat and even on submarines and in close quarters with men. Abortions can be made available to solve problem pregnancies. How will men ultimately treat females who give themselves without commitment and who are not to be rescued by men, but are themselves in the foxhole? We now have women boxers, mixed gender team sports and the elimination of separate boys and girls clubs.

Torah gives us a completely different vision that fits our nature. We lose the right perception of this nature and live a life that is not joyful and fitting when we lose God. Short-term pleasures are chosen, but lead to long-term emptiness and psychological pain that never ends. The Torah requires good ecology that nature may bless us and that we may bless nature. However, it is our dignity as created in his image and his command that lead us to so manage the earth. Animals are appreciated at all levels of being, but those with more differentiated consciousness are to be especially appreciated.

However, a fetus is a developing human person, created in God's image. It is a crime to take pre-born life and kill it. Men are usually focused outward for provision. Women with small children are then freed to give birth and to nurture infants. There are different biblical laws for men and women throughout the Torah and the New Covenant Scriptures.

Envy, jealousy, hatred, unhealed hurts and more provide the soil of anti-human, unbiblical philosophies that produce leveling. Leveling produces a bland, unhappy, dull existence. Instead of discovering our calling in our gifts and talents, we seek to see all become equal in income, recognition, rank and opportunity. Some of this quest for equality is good. Many have been oppressed in societal structures and castes that have nothing to do with biblical distinctions. However, others seek to obliterate the distinction between men and women, adults and children, man and animal, and even appropriateness in sexual attractions.

Once again, we note that the Torah provides us with the patterns of life that maximize mutual blessing. From Torah, we learn as well to distinguish time. Thereby we bless special times and seasons in God and are enriched by God from the patterns of life that make time special. In the Bible we have new moons and Sabbaths and feasts. Time is sanctified and provides a means of blessing God for provision and enjoying our place in his love. In memory of what God has done connected to designated times, and in prophetic foreshadowing concerning what God will yet do, we enrich all of life with meaning. God blesses us with feasts, and we bless God in the feasts! We see a similar pattern in the Church calendar, although specific days and meanings are somewhat changed.

Time is also marked by rites of passage. We bring blessing to God and are blessed by God when birth is sanctified in the dedication of the child. This includes circumcision for Jewish born males. Naming should again take on some prophetic significance as a blessing to the child and not just appreciation for the sound of syllables. The passage from childhood to adulthood and the consequent ability to produce children are marked in most cultures. In Judaism this is *Bar or Bat Mitzvah*. The child is blessed to become a son or daughter of the commandment, of the covenant. This is a prophetic blessing and a reception by the young adult of responsibility and the blessing offered. He also blesses God in his commitment. Confirmation in Church tradition is similar in function. Marriage has been discussed, but is also an important rite of passage wherein we see and affirm the order of mutual blessing to one another and to and from God. Even death is a rite of passage that is made special even if profoundly painful. We affirm the blessing that the person has been to us. We bless them and affirm their passage to heaven and the hope of the Age to Come. In addition, we bless God who is good. Even in the face of tragedy, we affirm that God will someday provide a restoration that will make up for all the seemingly unfair tragedies of human existence. This is the meaning of reciting the prayer of blessing, the *Kaddish*, in the time of grief. We bless him in the midst of death, and He blesses us with comfort and hope. Words sanctify the passage from this life and sanctify the burial. In Judaism eleven months of saying *Kaddish* are part of the praise to God that brings healing to those left behind. Because we believe the person continues to exist after death,

I refuse to speak in the common terms such as "We buried John." No, you did not burry John, you buried his body, but he is not there.

Beyond this, the Bible and Jewish tradition teach that good deeds, *mitzvot,* done in faith bring blessing to God and one another. Good deeds done in love and kindness also bring God's blessing to the one who does the good deed. Human life is to be filled with good deeds of love and seeking justice for all, the order of God's righteousness where each person can fulfill their unique destiny.

Though God gives us the means for living an enriching life in this age, we yet live in a world of tragedy. There are premature deaths, suffering, war and betrayal. Nature itself is fallen and sometimes turns against itself, even without human destructive behavior! Thus we read in Romans 8 that the whole creation groans and travails waiting for redemption and the manifestation of the Sons of God. This is why nature is not pristine-perfect, and sometimes human action saves nature! Late 18th century philosopher Immanual Kant said that to be motivated to good in this life we needed to believe in three things: God, freedom and immortality, none of which he believed could be scientifically or philosophically proven. God, because he guarantees reward and punishment for our behavior; immortality, because we do not adequately receive rewards and punishment in this life according to our deeds; and freedom, because only then are we really responsible for our acts. But to what are we to be redeemed? Are we destined to float on a cloud with a harp as somewhat ghostly ephemeral beings? This leads us to an important area of consideration.

The Age to Come- The Everlasting State

We have been redeemed, but for what kind of life? It is the life of God's intention for creation, an order of infinite variety and experience in an order of mutual blessing forever and ever.

Some believe that the Bible teaches two Ages to Come stages. The first is a glorious age called the Millennium where under the rule of the Messiah, human beings not yet transformed to their glorified state will attain to an order of the knowledge of God and mutual blessing beyond what we can fully imagine. Scripture describes abundant crops, absence of disease, joyful weddings, world peace, and the knowledge of God filling the whole earth. It describes harmony between man and nature. (Isaiah 2, 11, 55, 60, 66, Amos 9, Joel 3). The Isaiah 11 passage is just one of many.

> [6] The wolf will live with the lamb,
> the leopard will lie down with the goat,
> the calf and the lion and the yearling together;
> and a little child will lead them.
> [7] The cow will feed with the bear,
> their young will lie down together,
> and the lion will eat straw like the ox.
> [8] The infant will play near the cobra's den,
> the young child will put its hand into the viper's nest.
> [9] They will neither harm nor destroy
> on all my holy mountain,
> for the earth will be filled with the knowledge of the Lord
> as the waters cover the sea.

[10] In that day the Root of Jesse will stand as a banner for the peoples; the nations will rally to him, and his resting place will be glorious. [11] In that day the Lord will reach out his hand a second time to reclaim the surviving remnant of his people from Assyria, from Lower Egypt, from Upper Egypt, from Cush, [k] from Elam, from Babylonia, from Hamath and from the islands of the Mediterranean.

[12] He will raise a banner for the nations
and gather the exiles of Israel;
he will assemble the scattered people of Judah
from the four quarters of the earth. (NIV)

Some believe the Millennial age is only a symbol for the ultimate Age to Come. I believe in a literal transitional Millennial Age to Come. However, this is not herein my concern. Those who die before this Millennium will not live like the un-glorified but in glorified bodies. In the Everlasting Age after the Millennium, those who embraced God will all be glorified. Our question is, what will this life be like.

First of all, we must not think of the everlasting state as an ephemeral existence. Rather, as C. S. Lewis points out, it is a more real state. Indeed, as he describes it in his story, *The Great Divorce*, those who are not redeemed cannot walk on the grass of heaven. It is too hard for their feet. In another place he notes that Jesus did not walk through walls because he was ghostly. Rather, he walked through walls because the walls were ghostly to him in his higher and more substantial bodily being. Yes, the resurrection body is not limited as our present body, but is higher and more substantial, not subject to death and disease. I call this view the substantiality of our bodily existence in the Age to Come.

On this view of substantiality, I quote a question from the movie *Field of Dreams*. The star of the movie, Kevin Costner, asks a ball player from the Chicago White Sox team of 1919, "Is there baseball in heaven?" The answer is yes, that there is baseball! It implies baseball on a higher level. Why do I give this example? First of all, the Bible does not teach that the goal of human life is the soul's salvation without the body as in Greek and Hindu thought. In such a bodiless realm, it is pictured that the soul will just exist in a quiet meditative state of mind. For Plato, this is to gaze at eternal forms or ideas.

The Bible gives very little information concerning what life is like in the eternal state. Some have had visions of this life. These visions can be helpful. The Bible speaks of everlasting life in terms of a dwelling place of extraordinary beauty. One such description is of the New Jerusalem coming down from heaven. A group of Chinese children, at the turn of the century a hundred years ago, saw this as a pyramid with three levels and the throne of God on the top. The twelve gates of the city are all beautiful and decorated with precious gems. Upon the gates are the names of the twelve tribes of Israel. The foundation stones have written upon them the names of the twelve Apostles. The streets are paved with gold. The light of God is on the streets. A beautiful glow goes forth from the throne of God. On either side of the stream are twelve kinds of trees whose leaves heal the nations. The trees of life can now be eaten. This is highly symbolic. Then it describes multitudes that worship God in joy and ecstasy beyond description. The intimacy of fellowship with God will be beyond our present comprehension. Certainly it will be more than an everlasting choir or worship service.

Revelation describes the most important thing about the everlasting state and the New Heavens and New Earth. However, is this all there is? If God created a multifaceted world of amazing variety and endless discovery, can we think that the Age to Come will be less? Yeshua said that he would drink wine with us in His Kingdom. There would be a banquet. He ate fish in his glorified resurrected body.

My premise is that the Everlasting World will be one that is analogous to this world but without suffering, sin, disease and death. There will be more variety, not less, more arrangements of interdependence for mutual blessing. Not only will there be direct worship, but there will be worship connected to all we do since every act will be connected to seeing God. Every perception of everything will include the perception of God behind it. John Eldridge also has come to the same conclusion in his wonderful book *The Journey of Desire*.[1] Let us note some aspects of what I believe will be in this Age. According to C. S. Lewis, the Age to Come is full of the features of Old Narnia, the land of his stories (*The Narnia Chronicles*) but now redeemed in a New Narnia. There is continuity. Bishop N. T. Wright brings out a very strong case for the Lewis orientation in his *Surprised by Hope* on the resurrection and the Age to Come. I think it is the greatest book on the resurrection ever written. [2]

First will be fellowship or the deepest friendships. Our first friendship will be with God whom we will love with all our hearts and souls, with all our strength and mind. In addition,

---

1. John Elderidge, *The Journey of Desire,* Thomas Nelson, Nashville, 2000.
2. N. T. Wright, *Surprised by Hope,* Harper Collins, New York, 2008

the Bible speaks of our being reunited with our loved ones (I Thessalonians. 4:16,17). Those good and worthy friendships here will be even better there. Though there will not be a need for physical sexual expression, there will be an ecstasy in communion. We will know and love our spouses, children, uncles, aunts, grandparents, grandchildren and more. We will meet generations of ancestors who have come to know and love God. We will be able to share on so many things we can only then understand. We will converse with many people that we have longed to meet. There will be no lack of time to hinder us.

There will be a natural order. Those who have visions describe the most wonderful mountains, trees, streams, rivers, lakes, forests and grasslands. There will be myriads of flora and fauna to discover. Man will have a special communion with animals that myths and fairy tales have foreshadowed. Perhaps, we will be given the honor of molding some aspects of nature as the Swiss have done. Will the universe of planets and galaxies be for our discovery and development? Nature will be a source of never ending discovery and delight. The intertwined nature of it all will be more astonishing to us than that on earth.

There will be learning. I imagine that we will learn history from the divine perspective. We will learn the answers to our why questions. We will see the order of sowing and reaping and the real reasons history developed as it did. We will know the real heroes and real villains. There will be great honor to the honorable and disdain for the evil ones. We will see all the foolish deceptions of false philosophies and wonder how man could ever believe such falsehood.

There will be wonderful art. I imagine that the works of art that gave glory to God and wonderfully projected truth, beauty and goodness will be preserved. Why should there not be dramas to remember God's goodness in history? Why not new works of art to humanly give glory to God? Will we not compose music, paintings, sculpture and more? What will be the instruments for music in heaven? Will we create such instruments? Will there be a preservation of the instruments of music created on earth? What will be the infinite cultural variety that all can enjoy from many peoples and tribes?

Scripturally God has created a variety of nations so we might enrich one another with distinctive cultural creations. The wealth of the nations will be brought into the New Jerusalem (Rev. 21). Indeed, the passage says the glory of the nations! This cannot merely mean money. There is no need for money in this Age. It must be the cultural contributions and the unique aspects that are seen in every language and culture. We will be able to understand it all. The purpose of God creating different peoples is not that we will fear our differences or dominate one another. Cultures must be redeemed by the Messiah and judged so that what is good is preserved and what is evil is eliminated. However, every people have a marvelous contribution to make. God created varieties of ethnic groups, races and cultures for mutual blessing. It is that we might not have a boring world, but a world of great variety in cultural and personal discovery. So it will be in the Everlasting Age.

The following quotes from Dr. Frank Macchia, in **Baptized in the Spirit** are wonderfully appropriate and brilliantly stated.

121

The God of Pentecost self imparts in abundance and limitless expanse in witness to Christ, reaching out to all flesh in forces of liberation. . . The embrace (of God's love) does not oppress, force, smonth, or annihilate the others, but rather creates space for them in their unique character, and fills them with life abundant so they can be everything they were meant to be in all of their uniqueness. The tongues of humanity were not dissolved at Pentecost by the flaming tongues of God's holy presence (Acts 2:4). The diversity of human cultural self expression was preserved in all of its uniqueness and differences but caught up into a shared praise, devotion, and witness. God's freedom in this outpouring is a freedom to overcome all resistance and barriers to reconcile people into shared communion.[3]

So also Walter Bruggeman in *Genesis Interpretation:*
There is a dual edge to the scattering and diversification of tongues that actually fulfills the divine plan for filling the earth (Gen. 1:27,28). Such is God's plan for the free proliferation and diversification of a life that harbors no idolatrous illusions and finds its true dignity in glorifying God."[4] (p.97)

Will there be sports? There is no reason to believe that in the Age to Come that the talents and gifts in every man and woman will be the same. Some think that we will be able to do whatever we want. We will all be Michael Jordan in basketball

---

3. Frank Macchia, Baptism in the Spirit, Zondervan, Grand Rapids, 2006.
4. Walter Bruggemann, Genesis Interpretation, John Knox Press, Atlanta, 1982.

ability if we want to be. I do not see this. Some will be given to athletics in a new order. There will be the beauty and joy of the human excelling. Will there be team sports? Why not? Yet in that Age, we will not be selfish, but will rejoice in whoever wins, loving the nature of the game itself. We can no longer have good guys and bad guys. Those who excelled here and did so for the Gory of God may well excel there. Some may develop ability there with effort that did not have opportunity to develop here. We may have to ramp down our resurrection power type bodies to make this possible.

Torah will exist on a whole new level. It will not be external at all. Our spontaneous desires will be the will of God, the Torah perfectly written upon our hearts. New Covenant revelation shows God to be Triune. He exists in a state of everlasting self-giving in mutual blessing between the Father and the Son and between the Father, Son and Spirit. So differentiation and mutual blessing are the order in which all began and will be the everlasting state in which all will forever continue.

Imagine all of the personal stories to understand in heaven. Imagine all of the wonders of hearing those who triumphed and how! We will forever rejoice in the justice and love of God.

So this is the belief in the resurrection! Without it we cannot make sense of this world. With it, we see a coming order of creation, infinite in variety, distinctions of roles and being in an infinite varieties of mutual blessing. May God grant us the faith to believe in this world where boredom will never be known and where worship will dominate all our endeavors.

A Concluding Word on the Incarnation

This book did not concentrate on the theme of the *Incarnation*. In this doctrine, the Divine Son takes on human flesh and is both then truly divine and truly human. The incarnation, death, resurrection and giving of the Spirit are the means by which God cements or makes permanent the order of mutual blessing between God and humanity and the whole creation. Because God dwells among us, is actually incarnated in Yeshua the Messiah, the unity of God and humanity is forever established, a unity of mutual blessing and love. The death and resurrection of Yeshua assures us that in the Age to Come, the order of unity and mutual blessing will be wonderful beyond imagining. In addition, the giving of the Spirit to indwell us is a further establishing of an order of mutual blessing and intimacy between God and humanity that is beyond description. For those who respond to the Good News and put their trust in Yeshua, this mutual love, blessing and new joy in fellowship is forever. "For God so loved the World that he gave his only Son. ... The Word became flesh and dwelt among us" (John 1:16, 1:14).

AN APPENDIX ON LOVE

Love is a key to understanding mutual blessing throughout the order of creation. The whole order of mutual blessing in interdependence is a manifestation of God's love. We are called to love one another and all of creation, but our love has to be appropriate to the object of love in the hierarchy of value in creation. But just what is love? I add this little essay for greater clarity.

THE WORLD NEEDS LOVE

These words from a popular song reflect the fact that most people understand: there is something called love that is crucial if we are to see the world come into a better condition. Most understand too that love involves compassion for others. The song was not speaking about love as romantic attraction or adulation for another person. Yet, we find that many calls for loving action show that there is great confusion about the meaning of love, not only in the society at large, but among those who claim to follow Yeshua.

In the world outside the conservative Christian and Messianic Jewish communities, we find exhortations to love and to allow homosexuals to marry and to serve openly in the military. (The last has now been approved in the United States). In addition, we are encouraged to allow people to have no-fault divorces. Love compels us to have generous welfare and free high-tech medical services. Love seems to be bankrupting our country. The world also tells us that we should seek justice. Usually that is defined as equality. If men and women are not treated in the same way, or if income distribution is not more equal (how equal?) then we have an unjust society and such a society is not loving.

The Idea of Love without Moral Standards

The general idea of love in society is a debasement of the concept and often is mere humanistic sentiment. Society does not think—or rather, the people in society do not think—that love is connected to judgment or enforcing standards; instead "love" is taken to mean encouraging people to do whatever they want, when and wherever they want, so that they may feel personally fulfilled (as long as it does not directly hurt another). Today, enforcing standards is often considered unloving.

In some Christian circles we are encouraged to allow divorce without any eldership court to render a decision as to whether a divorce with an allowance of remarriage is justified. The pastor who divorces his wife and marries his secretary is to be embraced and allowed to continue in his role, for anything less is not loving or forgiving, and after all, it is said, divorce is no worse than other sins. But are all sins equal? Though any sin without blood atonement is enough to condemn us, is it just as bad to think of vengeance as to carry out the actual murder? Or is murder not worse than stealing? Biblically unjustified divorce is devastatingly wrong and has terrible effects on children and on our whole society.

God is Love

The Bible tells us that "God is love" (I John 4:16). It is the deepest part of his character. Yet it also tells us that God is a judge to be feared. In the book of Exodus we read the definition God's character that in the Jewish tradition is called the Thirteen Attributes of God:

> The LORD came down in the cloud and stood there with him and proclaimed his name, the LORD. And he passed in front of Moses proclaiming, "The LORD, the LORD, the passionate and gracious God, slow to anger, abounding in love and faithfulness, maintaining love to thousands, and forgiving wickedness, rebellion and sin. Yet he does not leave the guilty unpunished, he punishes the children and

their children for the sin of the fathers to the third and fourth generation."

Our purpose here is not to bring a full explanation of this passage, which clearly states that sin has inter-generational effects and brings punishment. This, I believe, is because evil behaviors are repeated generation to generation. Our purpose is simply to note that God, who is love and acts in love, also punishes sin.

A Biblical Definition of Love with Justice

So what is love? My conclusion after an empirical reading of Scripture is that "Love is the compassionate identification with others that seeks their good. Their good is defined by God's intended destiny for them." This definition has objective content, since nothing contrary to God's standards is love because God's destiny for human beings can only be according to his standards of righteousness for all human beings. This means that true love is guided by biblical law. Without biblical law, we are left to mere sentiment. A just order is one that enables people to fulfill their God-intended destiny, but an unjust order prevents or hinders the fulfillment of that destiny. Justice is not equality except in terms of those Scriptural norms where all humans are in the image of God, to be treated with respect and dignity and to be equal before the courts with regard to crime and punishment. Note as well, that this definition of love includes the place of emotion. Compassionate identification enables us to put ourselves in the shoes of the other and to feel an emotional compassion that motivates us to act for their good. Not all are called to have equal wealth as in a Marxist definition of justice,

127

but a just order must be one where responsible persons do have sufficient material provision since without that material provision, fulfillment of destiny is prevented. The definition also encompasses our love for God since love perceives the worth of the object of love or compassionate identification is not possible. When we identify with God as those created in his image, we are in awe of his beauty, goodness, love and justice and want to be part of God fulfilling his intended destiny for himself which is to see all humanity love him, submit to his rule, and acknowledge his Son Yeshua, our Savior and King. This destiny is everlasting loving fellowship!

This definition ensures the enforcing of standards. When standards are allowed to be violated, it inevitably leads to a whole order of injustice and sin which will end up preventing many from fulfilling their destinies and will destroy love. Love only flourishes in a just order. Children of divorce find it more difficult to fulfill God's destiny for them. A society that does not value marriage will lead to much destruction. Social orders where the powerful in business are in league with government powers and prevent real creative competition will decrease the wealth creation that will enable many more to prosper and to fulfill their destinies.

Love is not a mere subjective feeling. Love has objective content that is key to God's kind of love and forgiveness becoming manifest in the world. It is important to note that this ideal of compassionate identification with the other that seeks their good is only possible by the transforming work of Yeshua in our lives, by the power of the Spirit. He enables us to love.

OTHER RELATED RESOURCES

Available at Messianic Jewish Resources Int'l. • www.messianicjewish.net
1-800-410-7367
(Prices subject to change.)

Coming Soon! ## Complete Jewish Study Bible - New Testament

- The New Testament portion of the Complete Jewish Bible, adapted for the American audience.
- Introductions and articles by well known Messianic Jewish theologians including Dr. David Friedman, Dr. John Fischer, Dr. Jeffrey Seif, Dr. Dan Juster, Rabbi Russ Resnik, and more.
- Hebrew Idioms found in the New Testament explained by Israeli Messianic Jewish scholar, Dr. David Friedman.

Complete Jewish Bible: *A New English Version*
—Dr. David H. Stern

Presenting the Word of God as a unified Jewish book, the *Complete Jewish Bible* is a new version for Jews and non-Jews alike. It connects Jews with the Jewishness of the Messiah, and non-Jews with their Jewish roots. Names and key terms are returned to their original Hebrew and presented in easy-to-understand transliterations, enabling the reader to say them the way Yeshua (Jesus) did! 1697 pages.

Hardback	978-9653590151	**JB12**	$34.99
Paperback	978-9653590182	**JB13**	$29.99
Leather Cover	978-9653590199	**JB15**	$59.99
Large Print (12 Pt font)	978-1880226483	**JB16**	$49.99

Also available in French and Portuguese.

Jewish New Testament
—Dr. David H. Stern

The New Testament is a Jewish book, written by Jews, initially for Jews. Its central figure was a Jew. His followers were all Jews; yet no other version really communicates its original, essential Jewishness. Uses neutral terms and Hebrew names. Highlights Jewish references and corrects mistranslations. Freshly translated into English from Greek, this is a must read to learn about first-century faith. 436 pages

Hardback	978-9653590069	**JB02**	$19.99
Paperback	978-9653590038	**JB01**	$14.99
Spanish	978-1936716272	**JB17**	$24.99

Also available in French, German, Polish, Portuguese and Russian.

Jewish New Testament Commentary
—Dr. David H. Stern

This companion to the *Jewish New Testament* enhances Bible study. Passages and expressions are explained in their original cultural context. 15 years of research. 960 pages.

Hardback	978-9653590083	**JB06**	$34.99
Paperback	978-9653590113	**JB10**	$29.99

Jewish New Testament on Audio CD or MP3

All the richness of the *Jewish New Testament* beautifully narrated in English by professional narrator/singer, Jonathan Settel. Thrilling to hear, you will enjoy listening to the Hebrew names, expressions and locations as spoken by Messiah.

20 CDs	978-1880226384	**JC01**	$49.99
MP3	978-1880226575	**JC02**	$49.99

Jewish New Testament & Commentary on CD-ROM

Do word searches, studies and more! And, because this is part of the popular LOGOS Bible program, you will have the "engine" to access one of the top Bible research systems. As an option, you'll be able to obtain and cross reference the Mishnah, Josephus, Bible dictionaries, and much more! Windows 3.1+ only.

978-9653590120	**JCD02**	$39.99

Messianic Judaism *A Modern Movement With an Ancient Past*
—David H. Stern

An updated discussion of the history, ideology, theology and program for Messianic Judaism. A challenge to both Jews and non-Jews who honor Yeshua to catch the vision of Messianic Judaism. 312 pages

978-1880226339	**LB62**	$17.99

Restoring the Jewishness of the Gospel
A Message for Christians
—David H. Stern

Introduces Christians to the Jewish roots of their faith, challenges some conventional ideas, and raises some neglected questions: How are both the Jews and "the Church" God's people? Is the Law of Moses in force today? Filled with insight! Endorsed by Dr. Darrell L. Bock. 110 pages

English	978-1880226667	**LB70**	$9.99
Spanish	978-9653590175	**JB14**	$9.99

Come and Worship *Ways to Worship from the Hebrew Scriptures*
—Compiled by Barbara D. Malda

We were created to worship. God has graciously given us many ways to express our praise to him. Each way fits a different situation or moment in life, yet all are intended to bring honor and glory to him. When we believe that he is who he says he is [see *His Names are Wonderful!*] and that his Word is true, worship flows naturally from our hearts to his. Softcover, 128 pages.

978-1936716678	LB88	$9.99

His Names Are Wonderful
Getting to Know God Through His Hebrew Names
—Elizabeth L. Vander Meulen and Barbara D. Malda

In Hebrew thought, names did more than identify people; they revealed their nature. God's identity is expressed not in one name, but in many. This book will help readers know God better as they uncover the truths in his Hebrew names. 160 pages.

978-1880226308	**LB58**	$9.99

Conveying Our Heritage A Messianic Jewish Guide to Home Practice
—Daniel C. Juster, Th.D. Patricia A. Juster

Throughout history the heritage of faith has been conveyed within the family and the congregation. The first institution in the Bible is the family and only the family can raise children with an adequate appreciation of our faith and heritage. This guide exists to help families learn how to pass on the heritage of spiritual Messianic Jewish life. Softcover, 86 pages

978-1936716739   LB93 $8.99

Mutual Blessing *Discovering the Ultimate Destiny of Creation*
—Daniel C. Juster

To truly love as God loves is to see the wonder and richness of the distinct differences in all of creation and his natural order of interdependence. This is the way to mutual blessing and the discovery of the ultimate destiny of creation. Learn how to become enriched and blessed as you enrich and bless others and all that is around you! Softcover, 135 pages.

978-1936716746   LB94 $9.99

At the Feet of Rabbi Gamaliel
Rabbinic Influence in Paul's Teachings
—David Friedman, Ph.D.

Paul (Shaul) was on the "fast track" to becoming a sage and Sanhedrin judge, describing himself as passionate for the Torah and the traditions of the fathers, typical for an aspiring Pharisee: "...trained at the feet of Gamaliel in every detail of the Torah of our forefathers. I was a zealot for God, as all of you are today" (Acts 22.3, CJB). Did Shaul's teachings reflect Rabbi Gamaliel's instructions? Did Paul continue to value the Torah and Pharisaic tradition? Did Paul create a 'New' Theology? The results of the research within these pages and its conclusion may surprise you. Softcover, 100 pages.

978-1936716753   LB95 $8.99

The Revolt of Rabbi Morris Cohen
Exploring the Passion & Piety of a Modern-day Pharisee
—Anthony Cardinale

A brilliant school psychologist, Rabbi Morris Cohen went on a one-man strike to protest the systematic mislabeling of slow learning pupils as "Learning Disabled" (to extract special education money from the state). His disciplinary hearing, based on the transcript, is a hilarious read! This effusive, garrulous man with an irresistible sense of humor lost his job, but achieved a major historic victory causing the reform of the billion-dollar special education program. Enter into the mind of an eighth-generation Orthodox rabbi to see how he deals spiritually with the loss of everything, even the love of his children. This modern-day Pharisee discovered a trusted friend in the author (a born again believer in Jesus) with whom he could openly struggle over Rabbinic Judaism as well as the concept of Jesus (Yeshua) as Messiah. Softcover, 320 pages.

978-1936716722   LB92 $19.99

Debranding God *Revealing His True Essence*
—Eduardo Stein

The process of 'debranding' God is to remove all the labels and fads that prompt us to understand him as a supplier and ourselves as the most demanding of customers. Changing our perception of God also changes our perception of ourselves. In knowing who we are in relationship to God, we discover his, and our, true essence. Softcover, 252 pages.

978-1936716708   LB91 $16.99

Under the Fig Tree *Messianic Thought Through the Hebrew Calendar*
—Patrick Gabriel Lumbroso

Take a daily devotional journey into the Word of God through the Hebrew Calendar and the Biblical Feasts. Learn deeper meaning of the Scriptures through Hebraic thought. Beautifully written and a source for inspiration to draw closer to Adonai every day. Softcover, 407 pages.

978-1936716760   LB96 $25.99

Under the Vine *Messianic Thought Through the Hebrew Calendar*
—Patrick Gabriel Lumbroso

Journey daily through the Hebrew Calendar and Biblical Feasts into the B'rit Hadashah (New Testament) Scriptures as they are put in their rightful context, bringing Judaism alive in it's full beauty. Messianic faith was the motor and what gave substance to Abraham's new beliefs, hope to Job, trust to Isaac, vision to Jacob, resilience to Joseph, courage to David, wisdom to Solomon, knowledge to Daniel, and divine Messianic authority to Yeshua. Softcover, 412 pages.

978-1936716654   LB87 $25.99

The Return of the Kosher Pig *The Divine Messiah in Jewish Thought*
—Rabbi Tzahi Shapira

The subject of Messiah fills many pages of rabbinic writings. Hidden in those pages is a little known concept that the Messiah has the same authority given to God. Based on the Scriptures and traditional rabbinic writings, this book shows the deity of Yeshua from a new perspective. You will see that the rabbis of old expected the Messiah to be divine. Softcover, 352 pages.

978-1936716456   LB81 $ 39.99

Psalms & Proverbs *Tehillim* תְּהִלִּים-*Mishlei* מִשְׁלֵי
—Translated by Dr. David Stern

Contemplate the power in these words anytime, anywhere: Psalms-*Tehillim* offers uplifting words of praise and gratitude, keeping us focused with the right attitude; Proverbs-*Mishlei* gives us the wisdom for daily living, renewing our minds by leading us to examine our actions, to discern good from evil, and to decide freely to do the good. Makes a wonderful and meaningful gift. Softcover, 224 pages.

978-1936716692   LB90 $9.99

Stories of Yeshua
—Jim Reimann, Illustrator Julia Filipone-Erez

Children's Bible Storybook with four stories about Yeshua (Jesus). *Yeshua is Born: The Bethlehem Story* based on Lk 1:26-35 & 2:1-20; *Yeshua and Nicodemus in Jerusalem* based on Jn 3:1-16; *Yeshua Loves the Little Children of the World* based on Matthew 18:1–6 & 19:13–15; *Yeshua is Alive-The Empty Tomb in Jerusalem* based on Matthew 26:17-56, Jn 19:16-20:18, Lk 24:50-53. Ages 3-7, Softcover, 48 pages.

978-1936716685	LB89	$14.99

Matthew Presents Yeshua, King Messiah *A Messianic Commentary*
—Rabbi Barney Kasdan

Few commentators are able to truly present Yeshua in his Jewish context. Most don't understand his background, his family, even his religion, and consequently really don't understand who he truly is. This commentator is well versed with first-century Jewish practices and thought, as well as the historical and cultural setting of the day, and the 'traditions of the Elders' that Yeshua so often spoke about. Get to know Yeshua, the King, through the writing of another rabbi, Barney Kasdan. 448 pages

978-1936716265	**LB76**	$29.99

James the Just Presents Application of Torah
A Messianic Commentary
—Dr. David Friedman

James (Jacob) one of the Epistles written to first century Jewish followers of Yeshua. Dr. David Friedman, a former Professor of the Israel Bible Institute has shed new light for Christians from this very important letter.

978-1936716449	LB82	$14.99

To the Ends of the Earth – How the First Jewish Followers of Yeshua Transformed the Ancient World
— Dr. Jeffrey Seif

Everyone knows that the first followers of Yeshua were Jews, and that Christianity was very Jewish for the first 50 to 100 years. It's a known fact that there were many congregations made up mostly of Jews, although the false perception today is, that in the second century they disappeared. Dr. Seif reveals the truth of what happened to them and how these early Messianic Jews influenced and transformed the behavior of the known world at that time.

978-1936716463	LB83	$17.99

Passion for Israel: *A Short History of the Evangelical Church's Support of Israel and the Jewish People*
—Dan Juster

History reveals a special commitment of Christians to the Jews as God's still elect people, but the terrible atrocities committed against the Jews by so-called Christians have overshadowed the many good deeds that have been performed. This important history needs to be told to help heal the wounds and to inspire more Christians to stand together in support of Israel.

978-1936716401	LB78	$9.99

On The Way to Emmaus: *Searching the Messianic Prophecies*
—Dr. Jacques Doukhan

An outstanding compilation of the most critical Messianic prophecies by a renowned conservative Christian Scholar, drawing on material from the Bible, Rabbinic sources, Dead Sea Scrolls, and more.

978-1936716432   LB80 $14.99

The Red Heifer *A Jewish Cry for Messiah*
—Anthony Cardinale

Award-winning journalist and playwright Anthony Cardinale has traveled extensively in Israel, and recounts here his interviews with Orthodox rabbis, secular Israelis, and Palestinian Arabs about the current search for a red heifer by Jewish radicals wishing to rebuild the Temple and bring the Messiah. These real-life interviews are interwoven within an engaging and dramatic fictional portrayal of the diverse people of Israel and how they would react should that red heifer be found. Readers will find themselves in the Land, where they can hear learned rabbis and ordinary Israelis talking about the red heifer and dealing with all the related issues and the imminent coming and identity of Messiah.

978-1936716470   LB79 $19.99

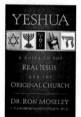

Yeshua *A Guide to the Real Jesus and the Original Church*
—Dr. Ron Moseley

Opens up the history of the Jewish roots of the Christian faith. Illuminates the Jewish background of Yeshua and the Church and never flinches from showing "Jesus was a Jew, who was born, lived, and died, within first century Judaism." Explains idioms in the New Testament. Endorsed by Dr. Brad Young and Dr. Marvin Wilson. 213 pages.

978-1880226681   **LB29** $12.99

The Gospels in their Jewish Context
—John Fischer, Th.D, Ph.D.

An examination of the Jewish background and nature of the Gospels in their contemporary political, cultural and historical settings, emphasizing each gospel's special literary presentation of Yeshua, and highlighting the cultural and religious contexts necessary for understanding each of the gospels. 32 hours of audio/video instruction on MP3-DVD and pdf of syllabus.

978-1936716241   **LCD01** $49.99

The Epistles from a Jewish Perspective
—John Fischer, Th.D, Ph.D.

An examination of the relationship of Rabbi Shaul (the Apostle Paul) and the Apostles to their Jewish contemporaries and environment; surveys their Jewish practices, teaching, controversy with the religious leaders, and many critical passages, with emphasis on the Jewish nature, content, and background of these letters. 32 hours of audio/video instruction on MP3-DVD and pdf of syllabus.

978-1936716258   **LCD02** $49.99

Gateways to Torah *Joining the Ancient Conversation on the Weekly Portion*
—Rabbi Russell Resnik

From before the days of Messiah until today, Jewish people have read from and discussed a prescribed portion of the Pentateuch each week. Now, a Messianic Jewish Rabbi, Russell Resnik, brings another perspective on the Torah, that of a Messianic Jew. 246 pages.

978-1880226889   **LB42** $15.99

Creation to Completion *A Guide to Life's Journey from the Five Books of Moses*
—Rabbi Russell Resnik

Endorsed by Coach Bill McCartney, Founder of Promise Keepers & Road to Jerusalem: "Paul urged Timothy to study the Scriptures (2 Tim. 3:16), advising him to apply its teachings to all aspects of his life. Since there was no New Testament then, this rabbi/apostle was convinced that his disciple would profit from studying the Torah, the Five Books of Moses, and the Old Testament. Now, Rabbi Resnik has written a warm devotional commentary that will help you understand and apply the Law of Moses to your life in a practical way." 256 pages

978-1880226322   **LB61** $14.99

Walk Genesis!   Walk Exodus!   Walk Leviticus!   Walk Numbers!   Walk Deuteronomy!
Messianic Jewish Devotional Commentaries
—Jeffrey Enoch Feinberg, Ph.D.

Using the weekly synagogue readings, Dr. Jeffrey Feinberg has put together some very valuable material in his "Walk" series. Each section includes a short Hebrew lesson (for the non-Hebrew speaker), key concepts, an excellent overview of the portion, and some practical applications. Can be used as a daily devotional as well as a Bible study tool.

Walk Genesis!	238 pages	978-1880226759	**LB34**	$12.99
Walk Exodus!	224 pages	978-1880226872	**LB40**	$12.99
Walk Leviticus!	208 pages	978-1880226926	**LB45**	$12.99
Walk Numbers!	211 pages	978-1880226995	**LB48**	$12.99
Walk Deuteronomy!	231 pages	978-1880226186	**LB51**	$12.99
SPECIAL! Five-book Walk!		5 Book Set **Save $10**	**LK28**	$54.99

Good News According To Matthew
—Dr. Henry Einspruch

English translation with quotations from the Tanakh (Old Testament) capitalized and printed in Hebrew. Helpful notations are included. Lovely black and white illustrations throughout the book. 86 pages.

| | 978-1880226025 | **LB03** | $4.99 |
| Also available in Yiddish. | | **LB02** | $4.99 |

They Loved the Torah *What Yeshua's First Followers Really Thought About the Law*
—Dr. David Friedman

Although many Jews believe that Paul taught against the Law, this book disproves that notion. An excellent case for his premise that all the first followers of the Messiah were not only Torah-observant, but also desired to spread their love for God's entire Word to the gentiles to whom they preached. 144 pages. Endorsed by Dr. David Stern, Ariel Berkowitz, Rabbi Dr. Stuart Dauermann & Dr. John Fischer.

978-1880226940 **LB47** $9.99

The Distortion *2000 Years of Misrepresenting the Relationship Between Jesus the Messiah and the Jewish People*
—Dr. John Fischer & Dr. Patrice Fischer

Did the Jews kill Jesus? Did they really reject him? With the rise of global anti–Semitism, it is important to understand what the Gospels teach about the relationship between Jewish people and their Messiah. 2000 years of distortion have made this difficult. Learn how the distortion began and continues to this day and what you can do to change it. 126 pages. Endorsed by Dr. Ruth Fleischer, Rabbi Russell Resnik, Dr. Daniel C. Juster, Dr. Michael Rydelnik.

978-1880226254 **LB54** $11.99

eBooks Now Available!
*All books are available as ebooks
for your favorite reader*

Visit www.messianicjewish.net for direct links to these readers
for each available eBook.

God's Appointed Times *A Practical Guide to Understanding and Celebrating the Biblical Holidays* – **New Edition.**

—Rabbi Barney Kasdan

The Biblical Holy Days teach us about the nature of God and his plan for mankind, and can be a source of God's blessing for all believers–Jews and Gentiles–today. Includes historical background, traditional Jewish observance, New Testament relevance, and prophetic significance, plus music, crafts and holiday recipes. 145 pages.

English	978-1880226353	**LB63**	$12.99
Spanish	978-1880226391	**LB59**	$12.99

God's Appointed Customs *A Messianic Jewish Guide to the Biblical Lifecycle and Lifestyle*

— Rabbi Barney Kasdan

Explains how biblical customs are often the missing key to unlocking the depths of Scripture. Discusses circumcision, the Jewish wedding, and many more customs mentioned in the New Testament. Companion to *God's Appointed Times*. 170 pages.

English	978-1880226636	**LB26**	$12.99
Spanish	978-1880226551	**LB60**	$12.99

Celebrations of the Bible *A Messianic Children's Curriculum*

Did you know that each Old Testament feast or festival finds its fulfillment in the New? They enrich the lives of people who experience and enjoy them. Our popular curriculum for children is in a brand new, user-friendly format. The lay-flat at binding allows you to easily reproduce handouts and worksheets. Celebrations of the Bible has been used by congregations, Sunday schools, ministries, homeschoolers, and individuals to teach children about the biblical festivals. Each of these holidays are presented for Preschool (2-K), Primary (Grades 1-3), Junior (Grades 4-6), and Children's Worship/Special Services. 208 pages.

978-1880226261	**LB55**	$24.99

Passover: *The Key That Unlocks the Book of Revelation*
—Daniel C. Juster, Th.D.

Is there any more enigmatic book of the Bible than Revelation? Controversy concerning its meaning has surrounded it back to the first century. Today, the arguments continue. Yet, Dan Juster has given us the key that unlocks the entire book—the events and circumstances of the Passover/Exodus. By interpreting Revelation through the lens of Exodus, Dan Juster provides a unified overview that helps us read Revelation as it was always meant to be read, as a drama of spiritual conflict, deliverance, and above all, worship. He also shows how this final drama, fulfilled in Messiah, resonates with the Torah and all of God's Word. — Russ Resnik, Executive Director, Union of Messianic Jewish Congregations.

978-1936716210	**LB74**	$10.99

The Messianic Passover Haggadah
Revised and Updated
—Rabbi Barry Rubin and Steffi Rubin.

Guides you through the traditional Passover seder dinner, step-by-step. Not only does this observance remind us of our rescue from Egyptian bondage, but, we remember Messiah's last supper, a Passover seder. The theme of redemption is seen throughout the evening. What's so unique about our Haggadah is the focus on Yeshua (Jesus) the Messiah and his teaching, especially on his last night in the upper room. 36 pages.

English	978-1880226292	**LB57**	$4.99
Spanish	978-1880226599	**LBSP01**	$4.99

The Messianic Passover Seder Preparation Guide
Includes recipes, blessings and songs. 19 pages.

English	978-1880226247	**LB10**	$2.99
Spanish	978-1880226728	**LBSP02**	$2.99

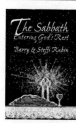

The Sabbath *Entering God's Rest*
—Barry Rubin & Steffi Rubin

Even if you've never celebrated Shabbat before, this book will guide you into the rest God has for all who would enter in—Jews and non-Jews. Contains prayers, music, recipes; in short, everything you need to enjoy the Sabbath, even how to observe havdalah, the closing ceremony of the Sabbath. Also discusses the Saturday or Sunday controversy. 48 pages.

978-1880226742 **LB32** $6.99

Havdalah *The Ceremony that Completes the Sabbath*
—Dr. Neal & Jamie Lash

The Sabbath ends with this short, yet equally sweet ceremony called havdalah (separation). This ceremony reminds us to be a light and a sweet fragrance in this world of darkness as we carry the peace, rest, joy and love of the Sabbath into the work week. 28 pages.

978-1880226605 **LB69** $4.99

Dedicate and Celebrate!
A Messianic Jewish Guide to Hanukkah
—Barry Rubin & Family

Hanukkah means "dedication" — a theme of significance for Jews and Christians. Discussing its historical background, its modern-day customs, deep meaning for all of God's people, this little book covers all the how-tos! Recipes, music, and prayers for lighting the menorah, all included! 32 pages.

978-1880226834 **LB36** $4.99

The Conversation
An Intimate Journal of the Emmaus Encounter
—Judy Salisbury

"Then beginning with Moses and with all the prophets, He explained to them the things concerning Himself in all the Scriptures." Luke 24:27
If you've ever wondered what that conversation must have been like, this captivating book takes you there.

"The Conversation brings to life that famous encounter between the two disciples and our Lord Jesus on the road to Emmaus. While it is based in part on an imaginative reconstruction, it is filled with the throbbing pulse of the excitement of the sensational impact that our Lord's resurrection should have on all of our lives." ~ Dr. Walter Kaiser President Emeritus Gordon-Conwell Theological Seminary. Hardcover 120 pages.

Hardcover	978-1936716173	**LB73**	$14.99
Paperback	978-1936716364	**LB77**	$9.99

Growing to Maturity
A Messianic Jewish Discipleship Guide
—Daniel C. Juster, Th.D.

This discipleship series presents first steps of understanding and spiritual practice, tailored for the Jewish believer. It's purpose is to aid the believer in living according to Yeshua's will as a disciple, one who has learned the example of his teacher. The course is structured according to recent advances in individualized educational instruction. Discipleship is serious business and the material is geared for serious study and reflection. Each chapter is divided into short sections followed by study questions. 256 pages.

978-1936716227	**LB75**	$19.99

Growing to Maturity Primer: *A Messianic Jewish Discipleship Workbook*
—Daniel C. Juster, Th.D.

A basic book of material in question and answer form. Usable by everyone. 60 pages.

978-0961455507	**TB16**	$7.99

Proverbial Wisdom & Common Sense
—Derek Leman

A Messianic Jewish Approach to Today's Issues from the Proverbs Unique in style and scope, this commentary on the book of Proverbs, written in devotional style, is divided into chapters suitable for daily reading. A virtual encyclopedia of practical advice on family, sex, finances, gossip, honesty, love, humility, and discipline. Endorsed by Dr. John Walton, Dr. Jeffrey Feinberg and Rabbi Barney Kasdan. 248 pages.

978-1880226780	**LB35**	$14.99

That They May Be One *A Brief Review of Church Restoration Movements and Their Connection to the Jewish People*
—Daniel Juster, Th.D

Something prophetic and momentous is happening. The Church is finally fully grasping its relationship to Israel and the Jewish people. Author describes the restoration movements in Church history and how they connected to Israel and the Jewish people. Each one contributed in some way—some more, some less—toward the ultimate unity between Jews and Gentiles. Predicted in the Old Testament and fulfilled in the New, Juster believes this plan of God finds its full expression in Messianic Judaism. He may be right. See what you think as you read *That They May Be One*. 100 pages.

978-1880226711	**LB71**	$9.99

The Greatest Commandment
How the Sh'ma Leads to More Love in Your Life
—Irene Lipson

"What is the greatest commandment?" Yeshua was asked. His reply—"Hear, O Israel, the Lord our God, the Lord is one, and you are to love Adonai your God with all your heart, with all your soul, with all your understanding, and all your strength." A superb book explaining each word so the meaning can be fully grasped and lived. Endorsed by Elliot Klayman, Susan Perlman, & Robert Stearns. 175 pages.

978-1880226360	**LB65**	$12.99

Blessing the King of the Universe
Transforming Your Life Through the Practice of Biblical Praise
—Irene Lipson

Insights into the ancient biblical practice of blessing God are offered clearly and practically. With examples from Scripture and Jewish tradition, this book teaches the biblical formula used by men and women of the Bible, including the Messiah; points to new ways and reasons to praise the Lord; and explains more about the Jewish roots of the faith. Endorsed by Rabbi Barney Kasdan, Dr. Mitch Glaser, & Rabbi Dr. Dan Cohn-Sherbok. 144 pages.

978-1880226797	**LB53**	$11.99

You Bring the Bagels, I'll Bring the Gospel
Sharing the Messiah with Your Jewish Neighbor
Revised Edition—Now with Study Questions
—Rabbi Barry Rubin

This "how-to-witness-to-Jewish-people" book is an orderly presentation of everything you need to share the Messiah with a Jewish friend. Includes Messianic prophecies, Jewish objections to believing, sensitivities in your witness, words to avoid. A "must read" for all who care about the Jewish people. Good for individual or group study. Used in Bible schools. Endorsed by Harold A. Sevener, Dr. Walter C. Kaiser, Dr. Erwin J. Kolb and Dr. Arthur F. Glasser. 253 pages.

English	978-1880226650	**LB13**	$12.99
Te Tengo Buenas Noticias	978-0829724103	**OBSP02**	$14.99

Making Eye Contact With God
A Weekly Devotional for Women
—Terri Gillespie

What kind of eyes do you have? Are they downcast and sad? Are they full of God's joy and passion? See yourself through the eyes of God. Using real life anecdotes, combined with scripture, the author reveals God's heart for women everywhere, as she softly speaks of the ways in which women see God. Endorsed by prominent authors: Dr. Angela Hunt, Wanda Dyson and Kathryn Mackel. 247 pages, hardcover.

978-1880226513	**LB68**	$19.99

Divine Reversal
The Transforming Ethics of Jesus
—Rabbi Russell Resnik

In the Old Testament, God often reversed the plans of man. Yeshua's ethics continue this theme. Following his path transforms one's life from within, revealing the source of true happiness, forgiveness, reconciliation, fidelity and love. From the introduction, "As a Jewish teacher, Jesus doesn't separate matters of theology from practice. His teaching is consistently practical, ethical, and applicable to real life, even two thousand years after it was originally given." Endorsed by Jonathan Bernis, Dr. Daniel C. Juster, Dr. Jeffrey L. Seif, and Dr Darrell Bock. 206 pages

978-1880226803	**LB72**	$12.99

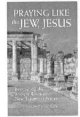

Praying Like the Jew, Jesus
Recovering the Ancient Roots of New Testament Prayer
—Dr. Timothy P. Jones

This eye-opening book reveals the Jewish background of many of Yeshua's prayers. Historical vignettes "transport" you to the times of Yeshua so you can grasp the full meaning of Messiah's prayers. Unique devotional thoughts and meditations, presented in down-to-earth language, provide inspiration for a more meaningful prayer life and help you draw closer to God. Endorsed by Mark Galli, James W. Goll, Rev. Robert Stearns, James F. Strange, and Dr. John Fischer. 144 pages.

978-1880226285	**LB56**	$9.99

Growing Your Olive Tree Marriage *A Guide for Couples from Two Traditions*
—David J. Rudolph

One partner is Jewish; the other is Christian. Do they celebrate Hanukkah, Christmas or both? Do they worship in a church or a synagogue? How will the children be raised? This is the first book from a biblical perspective that addresses the concerns of intermarried couples, offering a godly solution. Includes highlights of interviews with intermarried couples. Endorsed by Walter C. Kaiser, Jr., Rabbi Dan Cohn-Sherbok, Jonathan Settel, Dr. Mitchell Glaser & Natalie Sirota. 224 pages.

978-1880226179	**LB50**	$12.99

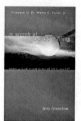

In Search of the Silver Lining *Where is God in the Midst of Life's Storms?*
—Jerry Gramckow

When faced with suffering, what are your choices? Storms have always raged. And people have either perished in their wake or risen above the tempests, shaping history by their responses...new storms are on the horizon. How will we deal with them? How will we shape history or those who follow us? The answer lies in how we view God in the midst of the storms. Endorsed by Joseph C. Aldrich, Ray Beeson, Dr. Daniel Juster. 176 pages.

978-1880226865 **LB39** $10.99

The Voice of the Lord *Messianic Jewish Daily Devotional*
—Edited by David J. Rudolph

Brings insight into the Jewish Scriptures—both Old and New Testaments. Twenty-two prominent Messianic contributors provide practical ways to apply biblical truth. Start your day with this unique resource. Explanatory notes. Perfect companion to the Complete Jewish Bible (see page 2). Endorsed by Edith Schaeffer, Dr. Arthur F. Glaser, Dr. Michael L. Brown, Mitch Glaser and Moishe Rosen. 416 pages.

9781880226704 **LB31** $19.99

Kingdom Relationships *God's Laws for the Community of Faith*
—Dr. Ron Moseley

Dr. Ron Moseley's Yeshua: A Guide to the Real Jesus and the Original Church has taught thousands of people about the Jewishness of not only Yeshua, but of the first followers of the Messiah.

In this work, Moseley focuses on the teaching of Torah -- the Five Books of Moses -- tapping into truths that greatly help modern-day members of the community of faith.

The first section explains the relationship of both the Jewish people and Christians to the Kingdom of God. The second section lists the laws that are applicable to a non-Jew living in the twenty-first century and outside of the land of Israel.

This book is needed because these little known laws of God's Kingdom were, according to Yeshua, the most salient features of the first-century community of believers. Yeshua even warned that anyone breaking these laws would be least in the Kingdom (Matt. 5:19). Additionally, these laws will be the basis for judgment at the end of every believer's life. 64 pages.

978-1880226841 **LB37** $8.99

Train Up A Child *Successful Parenting For The Next Generation*
—Dr. Daniel L. Switzer

The author, former principal of Ets Chaiyim Messianic Jewish Day School, and father of four, combines solid biblical teaching with Jewish sources on child raising, focusing on the biblical holy days, giving fresh insight into fulfilling the role of parent. 188 pages. Endorsed by Dr. David J. Rudolph, Paul Lieberman, and Dr. David H. Stern.

978-1880226377 **LB64** $12.99

Fire on the Mountain - *Past Renewals, Present Revivals and the Coming Return of Israel*
—Dr. Louis Goldberg

The term "revival" is often used to describe a person or congregation turning to God. Is this something that "just happens," or can it be brought about? Dr. Louis Goldberg, author and former professor of Hebrew and Jewish Studies at Moody Bible Institute, examines real revivals that took place in Bible times and applies them to today. 268 pages.

978-1880226858   **LB38** $15.99

Voices of Messianic Judaism *Confronting Critical Issues Facing a Maturing Movement*
—General Editor Rabbi Dan Cohn-Sherbok

Many of the best minds of the Messianic Jewish movement contributed their thoughts to this collection of 29 substantive articles. Challenging questions are debated: The involvement of Gentiles in Messianic Judaism? How should outreach be accomplished? Liturgy or not? Intermarriage? 256 pages.

978-1880226933   **LB46** $15.99

The Enduring Paradox *Exploratory Essays in Messianic Judaism*
—General Editor Dr. John Fischer

Yeshua and his Jewish followers began a new movement—Messianic Judaism—2,000 years ago. In the 20th century, it was reborn. Now, at the beginning of the 21st century, it is maturing. Twelve essays from top contributors to the theology of this vital movement of God, including: Dr. Walter C. Kaiser, Dr. David H. Stern, and Dr. John Fischer. 196 pages.

978-1880226902   **LB43** $13.99

The World To Come *A Portal to Heaven on Earth*
—Derek Leman

An insightful book, exposing fallacies and false teachings surrounding this extremely important subject... paints a hopeful picture of the future and dispels many non-biblical notions. Intriguing chapters: Magic and Desire, The Vision of the Prophets, Hints of Heaven, Horrors of Hell, The Drama of the Coming Ages. Offers a fresh, but old, perspective on the world to come, as it interacts with the prophets of Israel and the Bible. 110 pages.

978-1880226049   **LB67**   .$9.99

Hebrews Through a Hebrew's Eyes
—Dr. Stuart Sacks

Written to first-century Messianic Jews, this epistle, understood through Jewish eyes, edifies and encourages all. 119 pages. Endorsed by Dr. R.C. Sproul and James M. Boice.

978-1880226612   **LB23** $10.99

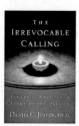

The Irrevocable Calling *Israel's Role As A Light To The Nations*
—Daniel C. Juster, Th.D.

Referring to the chosen-ness of the Jewish people, Paul, the Apostle, wrote "For God's free gifts and his calling are irrevocable" (Rom. 11:29). This messenger to the Gentiles understood the unique calling of his people, Israel. So does Dr. Daniel Juster, President of Tikkun Ministries Int'l. In *The Irrevocable Calling*, he expands Paul's words, showing how Israel was uniquely chosen to bless the world and how these blessings can be enjoyed today. Endorsed by Dr. Jack Hayford, Mike Bickle and Don Finto. 64 pages.

978-1880226346   **LB66** $8.99

Are There Two Ways of Atonement?
—Dr. Louis Goldberg

Here Dr. Louis Goldberg, long-time professor of Jewish Studies at Moody Bible Institute, exposes the dangerous doctrine of Two-Covenant Theology. 32 pages.

978-1880226056   **LB12** $ 4.99

Awakening *Articles and Stories About Jews and Yeshua*
—Arranged by Anna Portnov

Articles, testimonies, and stories about Jewish people and their relationship with God, Israel, and the Messiah. Includes the effective tract, "The Most Famous Jew of All." One of our best anthologies for witnessing to Jewish people. Let this book witness for you! Russian version also available. 110 pages.

English	978-1880226094	**LB15**	$ 6.99
Russian	978-1880226018	**LB14**	$ 6.99

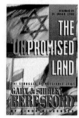

The Unpromised Land *The Struggle of Messianic Jews Gary and Shirley Beresford*
—Linda Alexander

They felt God calling them to live in Israel, the Promised Land. Wanting nothing more than to live quietly and grow old together in the country of refuge for all Jewish people, little did they suspect what events would follow to try their faith. The fight to make *aliyah*, to claim their rightful inheritance in the Promised Land, became a battle waged not only for themselves, but also for Messianic Jews all over the world that wish to return to the Jewish homeland. Here is the true saga of the Beresford's journey to the land of their forefathers. 216 pages.

978-1880226568   **LB19** $ 9.99

Death of Messiah *Twenty fascinating articles that address a subject of grief, hope, and ultimate triumph.*
—Edited by Kai Kjaer-Hansen

This compilation, written by well-known Jewish believers, addresses the issue of Messiah and offers proof that Yeshua—the true Messiah—not only died, but also was resurrected! 160 pages.

978-1880226582   **LB20** $ 8.99

Beloved Dissident *(A Novel)*
—Laurel West

A gripping story of human relationships, passionate love, faith, and spiritual testing. Set in the world of high finance, intrigue, and international terrorism, the lives of David, Jonathan, and Leah intermingle on many levels--especially their relationships with one another and with God. As the two men tangle with each other in a rising whirlwind of excitement and danger, each hopes to win the fight for Leah's love. One of these rivals will move Leah to a level of commitment and love she has never imagined--or dared to dream. Whom will she choose? 256 pages.

978-1880226766   **LB33** $ 9.99

Sudden Terror
—Dr. David Friedman

Exposes the hidden agenda of militant Islam. The author, a former member of the Israel Defense Forces, provides eye-opening information needed in today's dangerous world.

Dr. David Friedman recounts his experiences confronting terrorism; analyzes the biblical roots of the conflict between Israel and Islam; provides an overview of early Islam; demonstrates how the United States and Israel are bound together by a common enemy; and shows how to cope with terrorism and conquer fear. The culmination of many years of research and personal experiences. This expose will prepare you for what's to come! 160 pages.

978-1880226155   **LB49** $ 9.99

It is Good! *Growing Up in a Messianic Family*
—Steffi Rubin

Growing up in a Messianic Jewish family. Meet Tovah! Tovah (Hebrew for "Good") is growing up in a Messianic Jewish home, learning the meaning of God's special days. Ideal for young children, it teaches the biblical holidays and celebrates faith in Yeshua. 32 pages to read & color.

978-1880226063   **LB11** $ 4.99